WELL
BEING

About the Author

Dr. Jill Henry, EdD, PT, APP, is a full-time writer, student, practitioner, and teacher in the metaphysical and alternative healing fields. She owns and operates a metaphysical store, a website, and Labyrinth Park. She conducts seminars, workshops, and lectures on energy healing, self-development, and self-improvement, focusing on translating the new paradigm of energy medicine into comprehensible and practical terms for health care professionals and the general public.

© Jill Henry

Jill earned her EdD in adult education at the University of Georgia for her research on development and learning for transformation. She is a certified associate polarity practitioner and a semi-retired licensed physical therapist, and she is trained in basic hypnosis, chi gong, meditation, distant treatment, experiential learning, and adult problem-solving. She was a grant consultant for Allied Health programs and provided continuing education workshops approved for nurses, physical therapists, massage therapists, and bodyworkers in therapeutic energy techniques. Jill is active in the holistic healing field, currently constructing an Earth Bag Community Building at the Otto Labyrinth Park, where everything from drumming and sound healing sessions to bluegrass and harp concerts may have a venue to share.

As a business owner, Jill designs and maintains a metaphysical website (mountainvalleycenter.com), a training-the-trainer website (cfalpro.com), a well-being website (resourcesforwellbeing.com), a storefront (Mountain Valley Center), and the Otto Labyrinth Park in the mountains of Western North Carolina. Jill uses guided imagery to assist participants in balancing energy during group labyrinth walks in Labyrinth Park, an outdoor seven-circuit stone labyrinth on two acres set between creeks and lily ponds and old growth laurel forest. She has produced and recorded guided imagery videos on chakras, polarity balancing, and energy shifting.

Jill works locally with clients using polarity therapy, feng shui design, past-life regressions, aura biofeedback, and the tarot. She combines many of these modalities in her practice of distant treatment of the energy body and offers classes and consultations. She is a contributing author to various metaphysical magazines, with published articles including such topics as polarity energy balancing, exploring the energy of the chakras, and relaxation and meditation as tools for change.

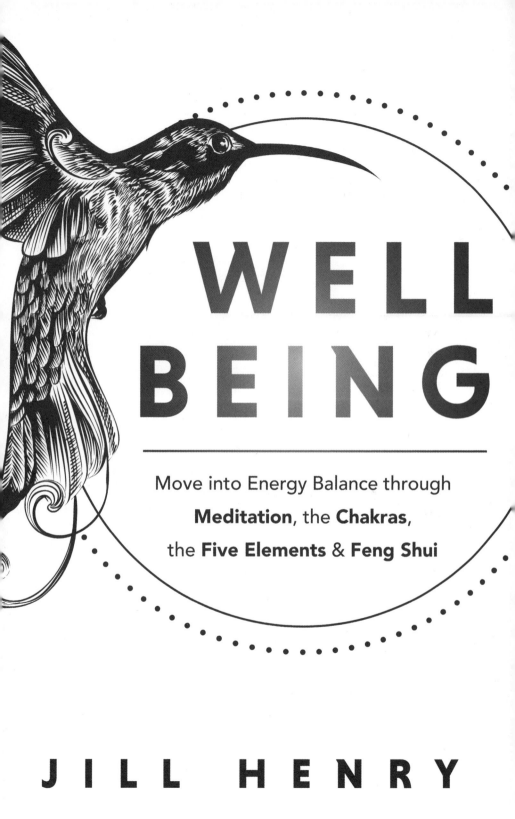

WELL BEING

Move into Energy Balance through
Meditation, the **Chakras**,
the **Five Elements** & **Feng Shui**

JILL HENRY

Llewellyn Publications | Woodbury, Minnesota

First Edition
First Printing, 2022

Portions of this book previously published as *Energy Sourcebook* © 2004 by Jill Henry

Book design by Christine Ha
Cover design by Cassie Willett
Interior art
    Chakra symbols, elemental polarity cycle, element symbols, yin-yang symbol, baqua diagram, elemental feng shui cycle, elemental creative and destructive cycles (pages 83, 87, 92, 97, 102, 107, 111, 124, 128, 134, 139, 144, 149, 162, 165, 166 & 185) by the Llewellyn Art Department
    Yoga figures (pages 29–31) and chakra figure (page 81) by Mary Ann Zapalac

Llewellyn Publications is a registered trademark of Llewellyn Worldwide Ltd.

Library of Congress Cataloging-in-Publication Data (Pending)
ISBN: 978-0-7387-7182-3

Llewellyn Worldwide Ltd. does not participate in, endorse, or have any authority or responsibility concerning private business transactions between our authors and the public.
    All mail addressed to the author is forwarded but the publisher cannot, unless specifically instructed by the author, give out an address or phone number.
    Any internet references contained in this work are current at publication time, but the publisher cannot guarantee that a specific location will continue to be maintained. Please refer to the publisher's website for links to authors' websites and other sources.

Llewellyn Publications
A Division of Llewellyn Worldwide Ltd.
2143 Wooddale Drive
Woodbury, MN 55125-2989
www.llewellyn.com

Printed in the United States of America

Dedication

This book is dedicated to lightworkers and lightseekers. Once we have discovered that we are made of light and love, we realize that we are here to shine our light and love so others may see their own. And ultimately, we are here to discover, learn, and grow in light and love. May this book help others find and shine and grow as we begin to feel and understand who we truly are.

Disclaimer

The following descriptions, practices, and examples demonstrate how the tools in this book may facilitate your own healing. There is no intention to use them exclusive of conventional medical practice. This book is not intended to provide medical or mental health advice or to take the place of advice and treatment from your primary care provider. Readers are advised to consult their doctors or other qualified health care professionals regarding the treatment of their medical or mental health problems. Neither the publisher nor the author takes any responsibility for any possible consequences from any treatment to any person reading or following the information in this book.

Acknowledgments

Without the spiritual energy, guidance, and support of my husband, Charles Long Henry (1948–2020), this book would have not been written. Forty years ago, we began a spiritual journey together. The journey took us from professors in physical therapy at the Medical College of Georgia to entrepreneurs in the Western North Carolina mountains. Along the way we developed trust in the guidance of the unseen Higher Self and learned together how to replace fear with faith and love. Though Charlie is no longer physically with me, I am grateful every day for the life we shared together.

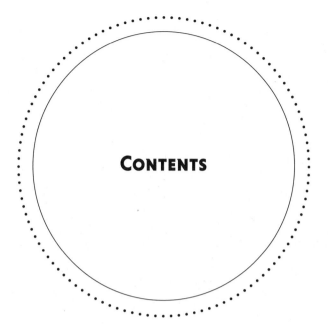

CONTENTS

Chapter 6: Using the Energy of Beliefs as a Tool for Well-Being   189

PRACTICES

Chapter 1: Understanding the Energy of Stress in Order to Find Relaxation

Chapter 2: Using Meditation as a Tool for Change

Chapter 3: Exploring the Energy of the Chakras

Chapter 4: Working with Your Mind-Body Type to Balance Energy

Chapter 5: Balancing the Energy of Your Environment

Chapter 6: Using the Energy of Beliefs as a Tool for Well-Being

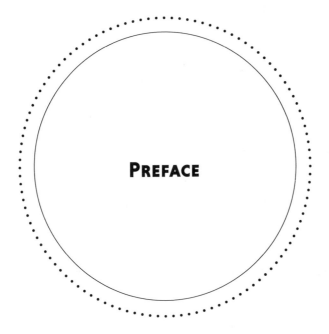

PREFACE

Well-Being was first published by Llewellyn Worldwide in 2004 under the title *Energy SourceBook*. It won a national award in alternative health in 2005, was translated into several languages, and was available until 2016. At that time the decision was made to not reprint. In 2016 I became the caregiver of my father with dementia and my husband with a brilliant mind and multiple medical problems. We owned a metaphysical bookstore and I also practiced part time as a physical therapist. Higher Self always provides what is best for us, and for those years I did not even think about republishing this book. Toward the end of that time, I retired from physical therapy and put all my energy into caregiving. I am grateful that I chose to spend the time with my father and then my husband while keeping my store and website income flowing. Those of you who are or have been caregivers to family members know just how much energy that takes. No one truly understands unless they have done it. I admire you most!

My husband passed in November 2020. It took me into May 2021 to go through the majority of files he left behind. Charlie was the keeper of the documents. It was then I discovered that I was missing all my files from Llewellyn Worldwide concerning *Energy SourceBook*. I emailed the company, and from that discussion, it was determined that *Energy SourceBook* may have been ahead of its time. The happy outcome is this revision!

The basic contents of the book are based on my dissertation titled "Development and Learning for Transformation" to earn my EdD in adult education from the University of Georgia. Time and experience have allowed this second edition to be richer and deeper than the original book.

About the Name and Cover

Long ago I spent several weeks determining and writing down my mission statement, my purpose here on Earth. I finally decided that my mission was to explore, facilitate, and advance well-being. To my surprise, this book's name turned out to be part of the mission I wrote long ago.

The cover was also a delightful surprise to me. When I saw the hummingbird, I ran to my books to discover what hummingbirds represent in our lives. Some cultures consider hummingbirds to carry the spirits of one's ancestors and lost loved ones. Well, that certainly fit! Hummingbirds' wings move in a sideways figure eight, or infinity symbol. That also fits, as the information you are about to read is truly timeless. Hummingbirds' hearts can beat as fast as a thousand beats per minute or as slow as fifty beats per minute, showing there is a time to move fast and a time to be still in our lives. Hummingbirds represent joy and happiness, bestowing gifts from Spirit of hope and inspiration that allow us to reach our dreams. May you dream high and reach your dreams.

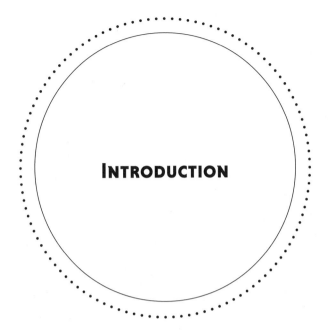

INTRODUCTION

My first career was as a physical therapist. The 1980s found me teaching as an associate professor of physical therapy at the Medical College of Georgia. I was awarded tenure and realized I needed a doctorate degree! My major professor at the University of Georgia asked me what I was really interested in. I said I wanted to know how people changed, not by willpower, but by a true and lasting change in perspective. My dissertation was titled "Development and Learning for Transformation" and it did transform my life.

As a result of my research for my EdD, I resigned my tenured position and opened up a metaphysical store. I invited practitioners to teach me and others what I only knew in theory from my research. My husband and I participated in a whole new world, and our energies and eyes were opened. Over the years we attended courses in yoga, reiki, tai chi, Silva mind control, mindfulness meditation, hypnosis, chakra energy work, and more at our store. We sponsored an interfaith group and learned about Hinduism, Buddhism, Eckankar, Science of Mind, Unity, and New Thought Christianity. Our study of *A Course in Miracles* resulted in a spiritual quest that ended up with us relocating in the Smoky Mountains of North Carolina in 1994. Since then, I trained in chi gong with a Chinese master, became an associate practitioner of polarity therapy, and was one of the directors of the American Polarity Association for two years. Along the way I also completed many craniosacral therapy courses, learned about frequency healing, and trained in distant treatment/healing. Today I continue to run my metaphysical store and website, offer on-site and distant energy body treatments, and conduct workshops at the Otto Labyrinth Park and Pavilion we created in Otto, NC.

Throughout my journey I have learned that every cell in the body vibrates in a frequency pattern. When the vibration is harmonious, the body is capable of healing. Stress causes the cells in our body to vibrate out of harmony, off frequency. This causes a breakdown in the cellular membrane, which, unresolved, progresses to a breakdown in the corresponding organ or system.

Stress can be physical (a sharp blow to a body part), vibrational (frequencies generated by our electronic devices), and mental/emotional (frequencies generated by our fears and angers). Mind-body and energy techniques and practices are available to help us relieve stress and allow our cells to vibrate once again in harmony.

In this book you will find over fifty simple practices to turn stress frequencies into harmonious frequencies that your cells will love! And all you need to do is find a few practices that work for you and that you can repeat daily. I will explain not only what to do, but why it works to do it.

You need no fancy equipment, no additional purchases, to discover well-being, just your own mind. I will show you how to travel beyond a limited, personal state of consciousness into the higher frequency realms of well-being and self-realization. There, the small ego self releases to the Higher Self and the path of well-being becomes clear. You may journey through this book chapter by chapter, or you may simply pick a chapter at random, read the theory, and practice the exercises. There are no rules, only understanding and experience. Many blessings on your journey to well-being. May your days unfold well for you always and forever.

The Meaning of Well-Being

Well-being is a state of physical, mental, emotional, and spiritual calmness and wellness. Life happens, but there is no need to grab on to it, to force it, to judge it. It involves the attitude of allowing rather than striving. Well-being can be experienced whether our bodies are perfect or not, whether our circumstances are perfect of not, whether our lives are perfect or not. The key to well-being is the absence of anxiety and suffering. If I have a physical illness or impairment or if I am in an undesirable situation, I can suffer with it, bemoaning to everyone, "Oh why me, oh how awful, oh how horrid." Or I can constantly stress about it, about what will happen and what should I do. Suffering and anxiety prevent the energy and feelings of well-being. I can have a chronic illness and still be well. I can have a physical disability and still be well. I can lose my job and still be well. I can lose a spouse and still be well. When we are in well-being, we tend to experience more health, prosperity, love, purpose, and fulfillment than previously. This generates feelings of gratitude for who we are and what we experience, which in turn leads us back into feeling ever greater well-being.

Well-being enables you, and me, to cope with and effect change in our lives and to improve the quality of not only our own lives, but also the lives of people around us.

Accessing the Energy of Well-Being

A state of well-being is developed by first understanding that a flow of energy and vibration underlies all physical and mental processes. Beneath the apparent physical, mechanical surface is a holistic, organismic flow of pure energy. This energy is constantly being directed by our thoughts, emotions, and feelings. To access this, to experience this energy firsthand, requires certain knowledge and skills. This book is a practical guide to developing those skills.

I have divided the book into six chapters:

- Chapter 1: Understanding the Energy of Stress in Order to Find Relaxation
- Chapter 2: Using Meditation as a Tool for Change
- Chapter 3: Exploring the Energy of the Chakras
- Chapter 4: Working with Your Mind-Body Type to Balance Energy
- Chapter 5: Balancing the Energy of Your Environment
- Chapter 6: Using the Energy of Beliefs as a Tool for Well-Being

3

Each chapter stands alone as a path to well-being. In addition, each section within those chapters stands alone. You can see the main sections within each chapter spelled out in the table of contents. Pick a section, read the theory, and try the suggested practices. The sections are short so that you may spend less time reading and more time doing. It is only when you are experiencing that you are involving your whole being. Just reading only involves your mind. Well-being comes from the integration of body, mind, emotions, and spirit into the present moment, where your needs are met before you know you have them and life becomes more joyous and loving.

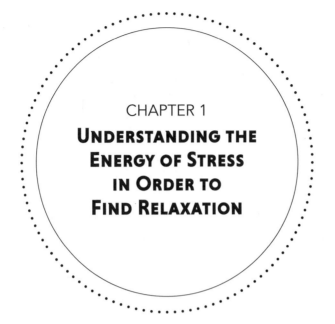

CHAPTER 1

UNDERSTANDING THE ENERGY OF STRESS IN ORDER TO FIND RELAXATION

Chapters 1 and 2 guide you through a developmental sequence of activities, from basic relaxation skills to deep meditative practices. You may choose to follow in sequence or skip directly to the section that interests you most at this time. The most important thing is to decide to do something with the information presented. Even if you only set aside ten minutes each day to practice relaxation or meditation, you will experience the benefits.

While working through these first two chapters, keep in mind that in Western culture, practicing relaxation and meditation is often viewed as wasting time. We have learned to keep busy doing things in the external world and sometimes may be seen as selfish when we attend to our own inner worlds. Yet it is our inner worlds that manifest into the outer. The more peaceful, happy, and confident you feel inside, the more you will have experiences of these in the outer world. Life truly is an inside job.

Coping Strategies for Stress and Change

Stress and change appear as a daily part of most of our lives. It is rare to meet anyone who doesn't feel stress over health or relationships or money, to name a few stressors. How we cope with our stress is the subject of this section. Notice that I have used the word *strategies* in the title here. Even if it doesn't seem like it, we are each responsible for our own emotions, not the other person's. Perceiving stress and acting upon stress is within our own interpretations of our life. We are not powerless here. I encourage you to look at how you cope with stress in terms of a strategy you are using and not a response forced upon you by the actions of another person or event in your life. This will help you clear your mind for the choices you are about to make toward your own well-being.

There are many strategies for coping with our changing world. Some are better than others. The best ones direct us inward as we develop relaxation and meditation. We will take a moment to explore some of the more negative and positive coping strategies.

Indirect Coping Strategies

Strategy 1: Drug and Alcohol Use and Abuse

This strategy is not highly recommended but is often used. Drugs and alcohol keep our anxieties below the threshold of awareness. If we are not aware of inner tension, then we do not have to do anything about it. That is, we do not have to grow and change. And that is okay too. There have been times in my life, most recently after the death of my husband, when a glass of wine before dinner was a perfect coping mechanism for me. It took me a while to accept that I had no choice but to grow and change into a new single life. Ultimately, that decision may come to everyone who uses avoidance substances.

Strategy 2: Psycho-physiological Illness

Illness represents a legitimate time out. It is a way to enter meditative states without guilt. After all, when we are ill, we have to stay in bed, and we are encouraged to relax and get well. Now, I am not saying that anyone, anywhere, consciously chooses to become ill, to acquire a disease, or to have an accident. I am saying that deep down in the mass consciousness, illness does represent a way out of our current stress. It substitutes a new stress for the old stress that made us sick in the first place, and it therefore helps us change. It is no coincidence that the word *disease* can be shown as *dis-ease*, or lack of ease in the body or mind.

Often when we experience trauma in our lives, we end up getting sick. Just being aware of this tendence may be enough to avoid chronic illness by dealing with the trauma and stress in a healthier way.

Strategy 3: Defense Mechanism

Defense mechanisms are attempts to get rid of stress by placing stress outside ourselves. Rationalization allows us to not feel responsible for, and therefore not guilty about, whatever it is that we think we should feel guilty about. When we project anger and blame, we are literally trying to throw our stress out of ourselves. Unfortunately, our stress is actually tied to us like a rubber ball, which comes bouncing back! Stirring up conflict is another defense mechanism often used. When we stir the pot, we hope to get the stress going away from us so fast that none will stick. Blaming others is probably not one of the best ways of coping.

Strategy 4: Escape and Avoidance

We try to escape or avoid stress by leaving early, avoiding peers, increasing isolation, taking long lunch breaks, spending more time with paperwork, or spending time in front of the TV or computer. The list goes on and on. I imagine you can think of several of your favorite ways to avoid stress right now!

Direct Coping Strategies

Strategy 1: Relaxation Techniques

Relaxation techniques are used as a principal means of coping when the environment is changing rapidly. They are used to relearn how to respond to stressful situations and include formal techniques like progressive relaxation, hypnotic induction, sensory awareness, meditation, autogenic training, biofeedback, visualization and imagery, yoga, tai chi, chi gong, and many more. We will be exploring many of these techniques in depth in the following chapters.

Practice
Eleven Quick Relaxation Techniques

This book is filled with successful strategies for not only coping with but also effecting change in your life. To begin, experience one of the following quick ways to de-stress and change negative energy into well-being. I ask you to experience it, because if you only read these relaxation practices, you have not experienced them. I encourage you to experience as many on the following list as you can. Perhaps you will find one or two that work for you and do help change your frequency from stress to relaxation. Go ahead and try one or two!

> *The Four-Count Breath:* Count silently to four while you inhale, and hold for four counts. Count silently to four while you exhale, and hold for four counts. Repeat for one to five minutes.

> *The Ten-Count Breath:* Count to ten! But do it so you are totally aware of each breath you count. If you forget to feel a breath, start over again at one.

> *Bodybreath:* Inhale through your fingertips, up the arms, and into your shoulders and head. Exhale down your neck, abdomen, and legs and out your toes.

> *Peacebreath:* Inhale while visualizing peace filling your body from toes to head. Pause, and then exhale while visualizing tension leaving the body from head to toes.

> *Groaning to Relax:* For five minutes, give yourself and those around you permission to loudly groan away the stresses that have been building during the day.

> *Laughing to Relax:* Take a laughter break—for five minutes, just laugh!

Muscle Relaxation: Tighten, then relax, each major muscle group in your body. Begin at the feet and work up toward the head, then progress to toes, ankles, calves, knees, thighs, buttocks, stomach, back, hands, wrists, elbows, shoulders, neck, head, and face.

Body-Mind Relaxation: Mentally breathe into each body part listed above, feeling warmth and relaxation begin to flow in each area.

Petting Animals: Find a dog or cat or another preferred animal companion and simply sit down and pet them!

Self-Imagery: In your mind, re-create a relaxing place you have experienced in the past. Return to that place and live there for a few seconds or minutes. To do this, close your eyes and picture a place you have been to where you felt completely relaxed. For me it is when I crewed on a wind-jammer sailing ship. For you it may be inside with a book on a snowy day, on vacation, or with friends. Take three deep, slow breaths. Release each one. Allow that image to form in your mind. Feel the air. Sense the fragrances. Hear the sounds. Spend a few moments there now. The brain doesn't know the difference between being somewhere and just remembering. While we tend to remember the bad things vividly, we usually don't pay an equal or greater amount of attention to the good. Permit yourself, just for this moment to feel good. Then gradually open your eyes, more relaxed than before.

Guided Imagery: Guided imagery takes the listener to a special place—a waterfall, mountain, meadow, ocean—and guides the listener through a series of releasing and heal-ing images. I've included the scripts for two guided imag-eries later on in this book: one in the guided imagery sec-tion in chapter 2 and the other in the chakra balancing section in chapter 3. I've also included some suggestions in the recommended resources section of this book.

Strategy 2: Music

All music has frequencies. Look for music that matches the frequencies of your goals. An example is the Solfeggio frequencies, tones derived centuries ago in the study of numbers (numerology), which are used today in energy frequency healing. Jonathan Goldman is a forerunner in both the musical composition of healing frequencies and chanting. Along with John Beaulieu, he pioneered the therapeutic use of tuning forks to generate specific frequencies. Examples of seven Solfeggio frequencies and their reported effects include 174 Hz to help relieve pain and stress, 285 Hz to help heal tissues and organs, 396 Hz to help liberate you from fear and guilt, 417 Hz to help facilitate change, 528 Hz for help in transformation and DNA repair, 639 Hz to help reconnect you with your relationships, and 741 Hz to help provide solutions and self-expression.[1]

Play relaxing or motivating music in the background. You do not have to listen to slow music to relax. There are pieces of classical music designed for inspiration, motivation, and productivity that energize while relaxing! Explore the type of music that relaxes you, then listen to it often.

Strategy 3: Exercise

Exercise is important to both mind and body. To gain the most benefit from exercise, it must be both regular and pleasurable. If your exercise is stressing you out, then it is time to learn the art of relaxation and apply it to your daily routines. We will look at the application of mindfulness to exercise later in the book.

Strategy 4: Diet

Ayurvedic medicine is a system of medicine practiced in India for centuries. Its aim is prevention by balancing and cleansing the body-mind. We will be looking at this system in depth as we discover polarity element balancing in chapter 4. Included in Ayurveda are foods based on the seasons of the year and *doshas*, or natural body-mind types. Because what we eat has an effect on what we think, and vice versa, we can look to certain foods to balance our stress. Categories of foods include:

....

1. Gaia Staff, "Healing Frequencies of the Ancient Solfeggio Scale," Gaia, March 14, 2022, https://www.gaia.com/article/healing-frequencies-of-the-ancient-solfeggio-scale.

Sweet: Sugar, milk, butter, rice, breads, pasta

Salty: Sea salt

Sour: Yogurt, lemon, cheese, vinegar

Pungent: Spicy foods, peppers, ginger

Bitter: Spinach, green leafy vegetables

Astringent: Beans, lentils, honey

You may find the following foods helpful when looking at stress or relaxation.

- To calm worry, fear, and anxiety, favor foods that are sweet, sour, and salty and reduce your intake of foods that are pungent, bitter, and astringent.
- To cool off from anger or frustration, favor foods that are sweet, bitter, and astringent and reduce your intake of pungent, sour, and salty foods.
- To stimulate and prevent procrastination and prevent resistance to change, favor foods that are astringent, pungent, and bitter and reduce your intake of sweet, sour, and salty foods.

Strategy 5: Changing Oneself

Changing myself involves the acknowledgment, without guilt, that I and I alone am responsible for how I feel and what I am experiencing in my life. No other person can change me or make me happy. A helpful way to look at problems is understanding that a problem can never be solved on the mental/emotional level on which it was created. If we knew how to solve our problems, we wouldn't have created them in the first place. We must look within our own consciousness for insights and strategies that help us think about old problems in new ways. Connection with our Inner Selves, Souls, Higher Selves, Inner Wisdom—whatever name you choose to use—will give us the ability to calmly observe our stresses and choose our responses without the drama we have been experiencing.

This inner work results in the emergence of a new level of consciousness, one that will not only enable our own lives to be better but will also enable us to help other's lives to be better too, just by being around us. Relaxation and meditation provide valuable tools for paradigm shifts, allowing us to let go and take control of our lives and our world in more positive and healthy ways.

Stress or Relaxation?

Relaxation is a choice we can make as we go along life's paths. It's important to know how and what to choose. Many people believe that stress is totally dependent upon their life situations. Some people simply have more stressful lives than others. To an extent, that is true. It is more stressful when living with too many responsibilities, being constantly dissatisfied, or having chronic worries. These three factors are influenced by our patterns of behavior and play a great part in our general level of stress or relaxation. Check yourself out on the following behaviors. Which category holds the most stress for you? Check all that apply!

Stress Due to Too Many Responsibilities

You are feeling stress due to excessive responsibilities when...

- ❑ You find yourself with not enough time to complete your work.
- ❑ You often become confused and cannot think clearly because too many things are happening at once.
- ❑ You become depressed when you consider all the things that you need to do.
- ❑ You skip meals so you can get your work done.

Total _____

Stress Due to Dissatisfaction

Your stress is coming from dissatisfaction when...

- ❑ You get upset when someone in front of you drives too slowly.
- ❑ Your plans depend on the actions of others.
- ❑ You become anxious when your plans don't flow smoothly.
- ❑ You hate to have your activities and plans disturbed by anything or anyone.

Total _____

Stress Due to Worry

Your stress is due to chronic worry when…

❑ You tend to imagine all the worst possible things that could happen to you as a result of whatever crisis you are in.

❑ You relive in your mind the crisis over and over again, even though it may be over and resolved.

❑ You are able to picture the crisis clearly in your mind weeks after it is over and done with.

❑ You can feel your heart pounding in your chest or your muscles tensing up.

❑ You have so many thoughts in your head that you actually have difficulty thinking.

Total _____

What are your totals? The area with the most checks is one for you to keep in mind as we move through this chapter because our initial attitude toward a life event determines our stress, not the event itself. To one person, a roller coaster ride is stressful; to another, it is a form of relaxation. We have learned to interpret events as stressful or relaxing from our families and friends. For example, to my mother, going on a car trip was stressful. What if the brakes failed, what if we ran out of gas, what if we blew a tire? For years after leaving home, I developed high levels of stress whenever I thought of driving away. Then two events occurred. I bought a car I loved and took a position at a university that required a lot of car trips. Between enjoying driving my new car and looking forward to meeting new people and seeing new places with expenses paid, I relearned to enjoy trips by car.

Think about some of the stress attitudes you may have inherited. Here are some that might come to mind:

- Waiting in lines is always stressful.
- If something takes too long, it's only natural to become upset.
- It is all right to lose your temper under stress. Everyone does it.
- It's not worth doing anything if I'm not going to win!

- It's better to do two or three things at once, like eating while working or planning while driving or bathing. That way, things get done!
- You should feel guilty when you are not actively working on something.

We can relearn by changing our perceptions about our life and our world. Perceptions are our way of making meaning and are based upon our beliefs about others and us. Changing beliefs and perceptions is not easy, but it can be done. In the coming chapters, we will take concrete steps to release old perceptions and gently acquire new ones. For now, it is enough to state that if our perceptions are non-loving, then we will experience stress. If our perceptions are loving, then relaxation is sure to follow, no matter what the life event.

I have experienced being fired from a job, moving to a new home, caregiving for an aging father with dementia, caregiving for my husband, and then the loss of both. Each one of those events was stressful, the loss of my husband stressful beyond belief. Yet I will still maintain that loving is the answer to regaining a sense of relaxation, safety, and peace. Because there is no other answer. To remain in stress for a prolonged period of time is not only unhealthy but also not a way to live a life of quality and well-being.

What does it take to change stress into relaxation? For me it takes a lot of practice. My toolkit includes yoga, chi gong, dancing, singing, inspirational reading, bodywork, regular massage and energy sessions, friends, daily (sometimes hourly) meditation, working, listening to music, and sometimes just watching old TV shows. Though the stressful event may not seem a choice, how we handle it is always a choice. Often my motto has been "I will not scare myself today!" I choose peace. I choose joy. I choose love. And I hope you will find in this book ways to choose the same.

Understand the Power of Your Perceptions

The present moment is our point of personal power. It is where we perceive and make meaning. A positive past makes it easy to see the future with optimism. A negative past tends to promote a pessimistic future. We have the ability to choose in the present moment, regardless of our past.

A pessimistic person views life through a dark lens of worry and fear. An optimistic person views life through, yes, I'm going to say it, rose-colored glasses. If there are clouds in the sky, a pessimist says, "Oh, it's going to rain and ruin my plans," while an optimist says, "Oh, if it does rain, it will be dry by the time I need to go outside, and in the meantime I'll do something else."

In the present moment, you have the power to choose an optimistic or pessimistic future. This is not denying your worries or preparing for the future. It's simply saying that you choose to move beyond them as quickly as possible. If I'm concerned that I will lose power in a storm, I get out the candles, fill a couple of jugs with water, and get out the pet travel bags in case of evacuation. I will not huddle in the house in fear of the storm coming. I will choose to see a future in which I am safe within my home and know that I am able to handle anything as it comes my way. The beauty of your choice is that when you choose optimism, you shift your frequency and create good vibes in the present and the present becomes the past of the next moment. Moment by moment we can choose to create faith, love, and joy. Awesome, isn't it?

Once we perceive an event to be non-loving, we automatically generate strong, negative emotions. Once we perceive an event to be loving, we generate calm, positive emotions. Traditional stress management is devoted to managing negativity after it has occurred. Our approach is to prevent its occurrence as much as possible. We will not neglect stress management, but we will focus on relaxation attainment.

The Choice of Stress or Relaxation Is Up to You

The choice lies at the level of perception. Life events occur. How you perceive events takes you automatically down the path of stress or relaxation. No one can tell you to relax once the perception has generated a non-loving emotion and its corresponding physical effects. You can choose to take time to work out of them and return to a state of loving.

Once strong emotions have developed, physical effects occur. Strong negative emotions such as anger, hurt, anxiousness, fear, insecurity, resentfulness, and general unhappiness can manifest as chronic muscle tension, increased intestinal disturbances, increased nervous system activity, increased metabolic demands, increased heart rate, high blood pressure, and decreased immunity—to name just a few!

Strong positive emotions such as calmness, happiness, friendliness, serenity, compassion, joy, and peace can manifest as relaxed muscles, free flow of circulation, normal heart rate and rhythm, normal blood pressure, increased functioning of the immune system, and natural body balance and flow.

There is a traditional Sufi story that goes something like this. There once was a man who had a son and was very poor. One day a wild horse came by, and the son caught it. The people in the village said, "Oh, that's so good." The old man replied gently, "We will see." The son attempted to tame the horse and was thrown off, breaking his leg. The people in the village said, "Oh, that is very bad." The old man replied gently, "We will see." As the son was recovering from his fall, the army came into the village recruiting soldiers. They looked at the son's broken leg and said they could not use him in a war. The village people said, "Oh, that is very good." The old man said, "We will see."[2]

Life is like that! When we can observe the story that is unfolding around us, with lack of judgment, which in itself is a loving kindness, then the drama and stress diminish. And we will see. The secret to relaxation has to do with staying in the present moment and letting a peaceful present generate a peaceful future, even during a storm.

When I find myself about to be in a stressful situation, I begin to prepare myself as much as possible. If I know there's a storm brewing, just like preparing for a hurricane, I mentally prepare. I increase the length of my meditations, and I focus on proper nutrition, breathing, and good night's sleep, so when the event occurs, I'm not on edge. I am able to observe both my reactions and the events of the situation. I've not mastered the art of no stress yet. In situations I find stressful, I still feel my adrenaline rising and know that there will probably be an aftermath I will need to clean up within my own mind and heart. The point I'm making is that years ago I would have given back that same anger. I would have been unaware of the storm brewing. Even now I would still feel the stress of the event and relive it long after the effects of the events are over. It's the over and over part that needs the self-love and stress management you are learning here.

....

2. Paulo Coelho, "A Traditional Sufi Story," PauloCoelhoBlog.com, accessed April 6, 2022, https://paulocoelhoblog.com/2008/01/30/daily-message-186/.

Recognize Thought Patterns: Worry or Affirm?

To put this into context, consider your first response to the following questions:

- When I get up in the morning, I most often think about

  _____.
- During the day, I typically think about _____.
- During the evening, I often think about _____.
- Just before falling asleep, I think of _____.
- On vacation, I most often think about _____.

If you are like most people, you answered the questions like so:

- When I get up in the morning, I most often think about what I'm going to do, have to do, or want to do today.
- During the day, I typically think about what I should have done and what I need to do.
- During the evening, I often think about what I didn't do that I wanted to do.
- Just before falling asleep, I think of what I need to do tomorrow and what I did today.
- On vacation, I didn't think about the past or the future. I was fully emerged in the present moment.

Our minds are constantly buzzing between past thoughts and future thoughts. It seems that only when we go on vacation that we can concentrate on the present—on the mountains or ocean or sunset. Four typical thought patterns follow. Can you find yourself?

Pattern A: Living in the Past. Always thinking about what might have been. Reviewing past events and conversations. Rehearsing what one "should have" said or done. Replaying past events while ignoring the present moment.

Pattern B: Living in the Future. Always thinking about "What might happen if …" and what I want or don't want to happen.

Pattern C: Living in a State of Confusion. Always bouncing between the loss and guilt of the past, pattern A, and the anticipation and fear of the future, pattern B.

Pattern D: Living in the Present Moment. Living in the now—the only point of action and personal power there is because there are no habitual patterns of thought.

The present moment is the only one in which to work. The problem is we have crowded it with our past memories and future longings. How many times have you relived past conversations, reviewing things you should have said or done? When this occurs, you are mentally bringing those past experiences into your present moment. You are inviting them into your home, your bed, just as if they were really present. And then there is the future, full of worry, doubts, and fear. Of course, the past may have good memories that are fun to relive, and the future may contain joyous expectations of good things to come. But they are still past and future and keep you from living fully in the present now.

Let us look at a prime example of living in the future—living with worry. Many of us learned to worry from our parents and have developed it into a fine art. "What if I fail? What if they leave me? What if I get sick? What if I will not have enough money?" Symptoms of worry include restlessness and feeling edgy, easy fatigability, concentration difficulties, irritability, muscle tensions and aches, and restless sleep. Chronic worry causes an imbalance in the brain chemicals, especially the neurotransmitters. Medical treatment for this chemical imbalance is often necessary to help the system become regulated. Once regulated chemically, it may be time to look for a deeper cause—the inability to control our own minds. Our thoughts are there, thousands and thousands of them. They are triggered by what we see, what we hear, what we smell, what we do. Our purpose now is to learn techniques to gain control of our mind, to choose new thoughts and to explore new ways of viewing the world.

The first technique we will learn right now is affirmations. We are affirming all the time. Every thought accompanied by emotion, belief, or expectation is an affirmation. The problem is most of the time we affirm exactly what we do not want. "I feel sick. I don't have enough money, I never get any rest. I don't like … I don't have …" Recognize any of those affirmations? What keeps our affirmations from being in the present moment is that we are bringing our past beliefs into the equation. And those past beliefs are guiding our future by their presence in our "now." Since at this time we believe we have to think something, why not think about what we want to have in the future "now"? And that is the secret of affirmations. To affirm in the present what appears to be not there with the belief and emotion that it is there, so it will be there! Sounds crazy, but with the right tools, affirmations can work for you. You are using them all the time, so why not change the negative ones to positives and see the results for yourself?

One of the most famous affirmations came from a French psychologist and pharmacist, Dr. Émile Coué (1857–1926). He was treating patients using mostly the same techniques as his peers, but his patients kept getting better faster. His peers became curious about what he was doing that they were not. Finally, they discovered what he was doing differently from them: Dr. Coué was giving his patients an affirmation to say over and over and over. The famous affirmation was *Tous les jours, à tous points de vue, je vais de mieux en mieux* ("Every day, in every respect, I'm getting better and better.")[3]

A more modern version is to say, "Every day, in every way, I'm getting better and better." Said with conviction and belief, this is a powerful statement, one that can make the difference between chronic sickness and healing. There is one caveat, however. If for every time I affirm "Every day, in every way, my life is better and better," I have fifty or a hundred affirmations such as "but I don't feel good now," "I'm tired," "I'm broke," "I'm lonely," and "I'm bored," then my negative affirmations tend to cancel out the positive. In addition, we often put more energy and belief into the negative than the positive.

In the 1960s and '70s, authors like Shakti Gawain and Louise Hay wrote about the power of affirmations. The movie *The Secret* brought affirmations into light in the early part of this century. Of more recent popularity is the work of Esther and Jerry Hicks, beginning with the original *Law of Attraction*. Since then, thousands of books, YouTube videos, social media posts, and apps have made information about affirmations common knowledge. What we affirm and believe often comes into our lives, whether for good or bad. It is about matching frequencies and the understanding that we are not isolated, solid beings but live in a frequency web with all other beings.

....

3. Émile Coué, *La Maîtrise de soi-même par l'autosuggestion consciente* [Self Mastery through Conscious Autosuggestion] (Paris, 1922), 12.

Practice
Develop Your Own Affirmation

Consider doing the following to experience the power of affirmations for yourself! To develop affirmations that work, sit quietly for a few moments and connect with your deeper, Higher, Inner Self. You will know you are there when you experience a sense of your mind becoming quiet and still. Then take out a piece of paper and draw a line down the middle of the paper from top to bottom.

On the left side of the paper, write "I desire…" and write down what you want to have in your life that you do not have. Now, for each desire on the left side of the paper, write down on the right side all the negative thoughts that come to mind when you think about having that desire, telling you why what you want isn't possible. And after each negative thought, say thank you. You are thanking the hidden thought for coming into the light of your consciousness and releasing it! For example, on the left side write your desires, and on the right side, write your pessimism, your "buts," like this:

I desire …	But …
To be free and clear financially and health wise.	It seems impossible for me! *Thank you.* I have so many bills to pay. *Thank you.* I'm so worried about my knee giving out on me—I may need surgery. *Thank you.* I'm not smart enough to make a lot of money—I don't have the skills. *Thank you.*

Keep writing until nothing else comes to the surface! Now do the same practice using "I can..." on the left side of the paper and continuing to list your hidden thoughts on the right side.

I can...	But...
Pay off my bills and be healthy again.	I don't know how. *Thank you.* I always get sick. *Thank you.* I don't have time to figure out my bills. *Thank you.* I don't have the insurance or money to see a doctor right now. *Thank you.*

Keep writing until nothing else comes to the surface! Now change your "I can" statement into an "I will" statement and then write next to it "because this desire is from my heart and soul. It is my destiny."

Often what is blocking your achievement is a deep, underlying commitment to meet everyone's expectations of you or an ego voice that says, "I'm not good enough." If you are affirming that you are not good enough in any area of your life, perhaps it is because of beliefs given to you when you were younger but that are no longer true now. Try writing statements like these with affirmations and notice how you feel.

- *I soon will have lots and lots of money, pay off all my bills, and have money to share with others because this is my destiny and soul purpose.*

- *I soon will allow my body to heal and recover from this illness because this is my destiny and soul purpose.*

- *I soon will find my soulmate because this is my destiny and soul purpose.*

Finally, become still and then write your want/can/will statements into a present tense affirmation.

- *I now tap into universal energy and allow myself to receive the abundance to fulfill my destiny.*

- *I am wealthy now.*

- *I now allow my Higher Self to guide me in returning my body to a higher state of health and well-being.*

- *I am healthy now.*

If you have gone through the process successfully, and it may take several times to do so, your final affirmation will carry with it a feeling of power and belief. And you will have switched from a wanting state of being to an allowing state of being. It is God's/Goddess's/Source's/Higher Self energy's good pleasure to give us the kingdom. All we desire is waiting for us to allow it to come into being. It's up to us to step off the garden hose and allow the water to flow. It's up to us to relax into our soul's purpose and know from deep inside that all good is coming to us. Begin here and now. If you still have doubts, no problem. Simply continue onward, decreasing the times you think or say the opposite and increasing the times you affirm what you want. Affirmations work by allowing them to work for you!

Use your affirmations constantly. Say them, sing them, write them, read them. Tune your subconscious mind to making it a habit. The affirmation becomes your first thought upon waking and your last thought upon going to sleep. And with infinite patience, watch your desires appear in your life!

There is an old song whose lyrics start with the message to emphasize the positive. That song is the secret of affirmations, of creating positive, present thoughts and feelings that will result in positive, wonderful future present moments. Good luck and good affirming!

Additional Techniques to Relax the Body

The body is not separate from the mind, and often we need to calm the body before we can calm the mind. Reminder: reading is not experiencing. Take some time to practice the techniques that feel the best to you right now. They may change over time.

The following techniques are all easy to do. The difficult part is doing them consistently. Any one of the following, when done daily for prevention, will result in marked changes toward body ease. When the techniques are performed only as emergency measures, they are less effective.

Breathing Techniques

Breathing techniques are used to quickly relax the body. When the breath slows down, messages are sent to the adrenal system that all is well, thus depressing the stress fight-or-flight response. Breathing with awareness can instantly begin relaxing body and mind.

Practice
Full-Body Breath

Try this now: Inhale, imagining your breath flowing through your fingertips, up the arms, and into the shoulders. Exhale down the trunk, into the abdomen and legs, and leisurely out the toes.

Place your hands on your abdomen, feeling it rise and fall as you breathe deep into your belly. Now count to three during each inhale, count to three while holding your breath, count to three during each exhale, and count three more while holding the breath. Allow the body to relax deeper and deeper.

Try inhaling for six seconds and exhaling for seven seconds, for two minutes. Hint: to count, mentally say a number and then a three-syllable word to equal one second, such as "one elephant, two elephant."

Practice
Alternate Nostril Breathing

To balance yin/yang, male/female, right side/left side energy, use alternate nostril breathing taught in some yoga schools of study. Place your hand over your nose, with your thumb on one nostril, index finger on the bridge of your nose, and your middle finger gently on the other nostril. Now close one nostril with your thumb, and breathe gently and deeply in and out through the other nostril. After a minute or so, reverse and close the other nostril, and breathe in and out through the nostril under your thumb. Let the energy move until it feels complete. Now, try alternate breathing. Close one nostril with your thumb and breath in through the other. Reverse on the exhale by opening the thumb nostril and closing the middle finger side. Now open the thumb nostril and inhale. Exhale through the other nostril.[4] With practice, you will soon find a soothing rhythm to your breath as you balance your energies through alternate nostril breathing.

Progressive Relaxation
"Progressive relaxation" was coined by Dr. Edmund Jacobson, who equated mental stress with muscle tension which, in turn, contributed to more mental stress.[5] He described the tense-mind, tense-muscle cycle and prescribed a technique to break the cycle and induce relaxation. The basic technique is as follows:

....

4. Melissa Eisler, "Nadi Shodhana: How to Practice Alternate Nostril Breathing," Chopra, November 4, 2015, https://chopra.com/articles/nadi-shodhana-how-to-practice-alternate-nostril-breathing.
5. Rena Goldman, "What Is Jacobson's Relaxation Technique?" Healthline, last modified July 21, 2020, https://www.healthline.com/health/what-is-jacobson-relaxation-technique.

Practice
Progressive Relaxation

Lie down, close your eyes, and place your attention on your toes. Bend your toes and tighten, tighten, tighten, hold, and now relax. Repeat two or three times until you become aware of the feeling of relaxation in your toes. Progress through every body part: toes, ankles, calves, knees, thighs, hips, buttocks, abdomen, chest, back, shoulders, arms, elbows, wrists, hands, neck, face, mouth, eyes, and scalp.

Return to any body part that still feels tense, tighten, and relax. Lie still and allow relaxation to flow through your body.

Autogenic Training

In the 1920s, German psychologist Johannes Heinrich Schultz developed a way to target the physical expression of stress, later called autogenic training. Autogenic training is a mental variation of progressive relaxation. Instead of actually moving muscles, you move energy in your mind. By directing energy to various body parts, you allow feelings of warmth and relaxation to occur.[6]

Researchers Erik Peper and Katherine H. Gibney led a study with 219 subjects (students) in a structured learning experience. Students were talked through several general relaxation exercises, then instructed to visualize the blood pumping from their hearts down their arms into their hands for seven minutes while holding the bulb of a glass thermometer between their thumb and index finger of their right hand. The results demonstrated the potency of the mind to move bodily fluids. They found that "the average temperature increased from 85.3 to 95.4 degrees Fahrenheit." Self-reported stress levels also decreased from 4.3 to 2.2

....

6. Arlin Cuncic, "Autogenic Training for Reducing Anxiety," Very Well Mind, last modified August 16, 2020, https://www.verywellmind.com/how-to-practice-autogenic -training-for-relaxation-3024387.

on a 9 point scale as a result of the entire experience.[7] If we can warm up our hands mentally, by increasing the circulation of blood into the capillaries, then we can use autogenic training to do this for any part of our bodies. As we think about a body part, we are sending neurological commands to that part, opening up both neural and vascular pathways. Our minds and bodies are intimately connected. More studies like this will be occurring as we direct our mental thought to the physical body, thus sending energy to structures and organs.

Practice
Autogenic Training

Imagine a ball of light and warmth, sparkling just above the top of your head. Bring this ball of energy and light down into your head and feel it massaging all the cells and tissues in your brain, scalp, and face with its healing light.

Progress the ball down through the head, face, neck, shoulders, arms, hands, chest, abdomen, pelvis, back, hips, thighs, knees, ankles, and feet. Allow the energy to circulate through your whole body. Feel the light shining away all darkness.

Allow the light to move through the pores of your skin, surrounding you in a halo of light. Gradually open your eyes and move around.

Relaxercise

Relaxercise is a series of ten exercises based on the work of Dr. Moshe Feldenkrais's method Awareness Through Movement.[8] Each exercise consists of gentle, slow, repeated movements of different body parts within a pain-free range of motion. These gentle, slow movements assist the body in releasing stored

....

7. Erik Peper and Katherine H. Gibney, "A Teaching Strategy for Successful Hand Warming," *Somatics* 14, no. 1 (2003): 26–30, https://bio-medical.com/media/support/teaching_strategy_for_successful_hand_warming.pdf.
8. David Zemach-Bersin, *Relaxercise: The Easy New Way to Health and Fitness* (San Francisco: Harper One, 2016), Kindle.

tension and regaining comfortable movement. The following provides a general idea of the type of exercise involved. Study with a certified Feldenkrais practitioner for the full program and exercise sequences.

Practice
Loosening the Upper Body

Sit upright in a straight chair with your back against the chair back. Slowly turn your upper trunk, neck, and shoulders all together to the left. Notice how far you can go comfortably by noting a spot on the wall behind you. Repeat this motion slowly, in a pain-free range of motion, six to ten times. Whatever speed you started moving at, now go more slowly. Ten seconds to move from looking forward to looking over your shoulder is a good speed. I'm really describing very slow motion. The slower you go, the more muscle control you develop and the less tension you have.

Now turn your shoulders to the left while keeping your head straight in front of you. Repeat six to ten times.

Now turn your trunk and head to the left, while keeping your eyes looking straight in front of you. Repeat six to ten times.

Now turn your trunk, head, and eyes at the same time to left. Can you see any farther behind you? Repeat the above while turning to the right.

Yoga

Yoga was derived from the Vedas centuries ago as one of the many paths to God. For years it was scorned in America because it was thought of as a religion. It can be a spiritual experience, but it also can be one of the best forms of stretching exercise a person can perform without any reference to culture or religion.

Yoga forms of exercise are remarkable for releasing tension and reducing stress. In yoga you assume different postures while placing gentle stretches on different body areas. Yoga postures are precise and have been used for centuries to relieve physical and mental dis-ease as well as to be a path to higher spiritual understandings. The best way to learn yoga is to find a good teacher in your area and take a class. Books and videos are available when you cannot find a teacher.

Practice
Yoga Stretch for Trunk, Hips, and Shoulders

The following is one example of thousands of yoga sequences. These moves are helpful in relaxing the chronic contraction of the abdominal muscles from the startle reflex and ensuing chronic stress response. When we are startled, we curl inward. Constantly being startled or stressed results in the trunk flexed posture of aging and old age. If you try this one, please stay in pain-free movements. If you cannot move the way described, go where you can as long as it is not painful.

Lie on the floor on your stomach (Reverse Corpse Pose). Place your hands next to your shoulders and gently lift up, allowing your stomach to remain on the floor, and stretching your shoulders and upper back (Cobra Pose). If possible, gently move from Cobra Pose into full Upward-Facing Dog Pose, lifting your stomach off the floor by straightening your arms, arching your back, and allowing the muscles in the front of your hips to stretch also. Spend a moment here allowing the front of your body to stretch from your shoulders to your hips. Do not push into actual pain. Feel the stretching release as it occurs in your muscles and fascia.

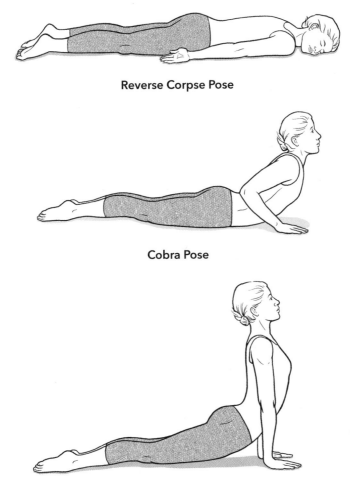

Reverse Corpse Pose

Cobra Pose

Upward-Facing Dog Pose

Next, push gently backward, lifting your bottom up until you are resting with your hands and knees on the floor in Tabletop Pose. Now push your bottom back so your bottom is lying on your lower leg calf muscles and your arms are stretched out in front of you in Child's Pose. Your buttocks may rest on your lower legs and heels, with the tops of your feet flat on the floor and your toes stretched behind you. Stretch your arms out in front of you on the floor. Completely relax in this pose for a moment. This is not an aerobic exercise. It is a practice that allows the body to move away from stress and into relaxation.

Tabletop Pose

Child's Pose

When ready, reverse the movements. Lift up into a hands-and-knees position (Tabletop Pose). Spend a moment there. You may even decide while here to alternate arching your back by relaxing your belly and then tightening your belly and rounding your back a few times (Cow Pose and Cat Pose). When ready, continue down until you are once again lying on the floor on your stomach in Reverse Corpse Pose. Breath, relax, and go again! Release the toes backward so that the tops of your feet are resting flat on the floor and relax.

Tabletop Pose

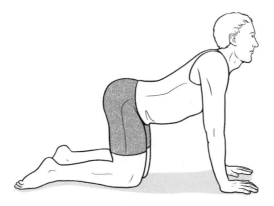

Cow Pose

Cat Pose

Reverse Corpse Pose

Repeat the entire sequence five to ten times, slowing and enjoying the stretch.

Tai Chi and Chi Gong

Tai chi and chi gong are forms of relaxation experienced by performing simple, commonplace movements in very specific ways. They are designed to facilitate the flow of life energy, chi, and release blocks. They require instruction, preferably from a master.

Years ago I studied in person with Master Luke Chan, a Chinese master of Chi-Lel Qigong. Master Chan studied at the then-largest medicine-less hospital in China, using only chi energy to heal 85 percent of admitted patients. Chi-Lel Qigong is an open system based on the idea of releasing all internal energy to the universe and absorbing fresh universal energy into the body and mind while using affirmations.

Practice
Moving Energy

One simple practice of chi gong is to sit or lie down and place your hands over your navel, palms toward the belly. Now slowly move your hands apart and forward while affirming, "I release all that is no longer necessary to my optimal health and well-being" and imagining releasing of energy to the universe. Then slowly bring your hands back toward each other and your belly while imagining absorbing universal energy into your energy field and affirming, "I am bringing into my life universal energy, chi, for my optimal health and well-being." Do this practice anywhere and anytime, for as long a time as you wish. Some days I've spent ten minutes, other days several hours.

Aerobic Exercise: Sports, Weight Lifting, and Running

Aerobic exercise, including sports, weight lifting, walking, and running, may or may not reduce stress. If performed with tense muscles or a tense mind, energy may be blocked instead of released. Attitude is all-important! If you enjoy it, do it. If not, find another way!

I recommend any exercise or practice you enjoy that is noncompetitive. By that I mean that you don't get tense or upset if you don't do it right or have not performed as someone else does. Being satisfied with yourself is one of the best stress reducers in the world. Here's an example. In high school I was a member of a citywide choral group whose sponsor produced a couple of albums. Last year I transferred the albums into MP3s. Most days I stand in my living room and sing along, with the same choreography I used as a teenager. It's great aerobics, lung expansion, affirmation, and inspiration all rolled into one for me. I enjoy it. I can do it at home or anywhere because I have it on my smartphone. And I feel better afterward. To some this may seem silly. To me it is becoming my most enjoyable form of exercise along with chi gong and yoga stretches.

Massage and Bodywork

Massage and bodywork are both ancient and common. To be a massage therapist in the United States requires at least 500 hours of training and a license to practice, varying by state. Many massage therapists have private practices, though some have joined forces with spas and corporate services. Other licensed health care professions also are trained in massage, including physical therapists and athletic trainers. Different types of massage, to name a few, include Swedish, hot stone, aromatherapy, deep tissue, sport, trigger point, reflexology, shiatsu, and Thai.

Craniosacral therapy, chiropractic, myofascial release, and even acupuncture fall into the bodywork category, which includes anything that is invasive or manipulative to the body. Most of practitioners in these areas are licensed after extensive training.

As a physical therapist, I have received or performed most of these techniques. The bodywork I use varies depending upon the type of stress I've fed into my body and whether it is acute or has become chronic. My advice is to look for recommendations from friends or coworkers in your area to choose the best match for you. Only go back and receive more treatments from an individual if you found it of benefit. All these techniques and practices are intended to ultimately de-stress the body, not make it more tense.

Practice
Self-Massage

The feet and hands are the easiest to self-massage. You can do a foot or hand massage with or without lotion. For a foot massage, cross one leg over your thigh so you can reach your foot with the opposite hand. Use the thumb of the hand holding the bottom of your foot to deeply rub the foot, from heel to just under your toes. Press down to find a sore spot, then rub your thumb in circles over that spot until you feel a release or lessening of tension there. Then move on to the next spot. It is not unusual to find many sore spots. It might be helpful, but is not necessary, to look at a reflexology chart to see what area of your body the sore spots reflect. Continue looking for and massaging spots on the top of your foot. Now rub each toe, from its base to its tip, stopping and using the circular thumb motion to ease the sore spots.

For a hand massage, the same principle applies. Massage both the palm and the fingers of one hand with the other hand, looking for sore spots and using a circular motion with your thumb to rub them. Be gentle. Sore spots are where the tension is being held. You can't untense if the pressure is too sharp or hard. Gentle, firm, even, loving pressure is best in self-massage.

You may give yourself a whole-body massage after your shower using sesame or almond oil, or try dry skin brushing to stimulate and relax the whole body. Buy a soft bristle brush and take off your clothes. Brush your body from your feet to your head to bring in earth energy for your day. Or brush from your head to your feet to dissipate unwanted energy, sending it out of your feet and back into the earth. The skin is the largest organ in the body. Brushing it is a great way to bring more well-being into your day!

Energy Therapies: Reiki, Polarity, Distant Healing

Energy therapies work with the body's energy system without manipulation of bodily tissue. Some therapies are hybrid between gentle touch and no touch. Craniosacral therapy, therapeutic touch, and polarity therapy use a touch so light that it is barely felt on the skin. Other therapies like reiki and distant healing do not touch the skin at all. The journal article "Distant Healing Intention Therapies: An Overview of the Scientific Evidence" describes these non-touch therapies as distant healing intention (DHI) therapies. DHI is defined as "a compassionate mental act directed toward the health and well-being of a distant person" and includes "intercessory prayer, spiritual healing, aura healing, energy healing, energy psychology, shamanic healing, nonlocal healing, therapeutic touch (TT), quantum-touch, chi gong, reconnective healing, Johrei, and Reiki."[9] It is beyond the scope of this book to provide the research here, but I will share what I believe is happening during distant healing.

Over the years I have experienced the aura, etheric, or energy body more clearly while working in person with clients. I have also experienced and seen results unexplained by not physically touching another person. Distant energy work with our energy bodies is gentle and effective. It energizes both the treater and the person being treated. And it may be another way of giving and receiving healing that is complimentary to conventional medicine. What if, during surgery, you had twenty people praying for you? Would it help? I don't know. Would it hurt? No. As we explore and understand that we are more than our physical bodies and that our physical bodies are made of energy, of frequency, distant healing comes more into consideration. To begin at the beginning, the first step is to feel and experience your own energy in the following practice.

....

9. Dean Radin, Marilyn Schlitz, and Christopher Baur, "Distant Healing Intention Therapies: An Overview of the Scientific Evidence," *Global Advances in Health and Medicine* 4, supplement (November 2015): 67, doi:10.7453/gahmj.2015.012.suppl.

Practice
Feeling Energy

Hold your hands in front of your chest, with elbows bent and palms facing each other. Gently open and close your hands as if you were holding an imaginary ball between them. Move your palms together and away, slowly, until you feel something between them. That something may be small at first. Become aware of when you feel it and when you don't feel it. You will start out by feeling it only when your hands are close together. Gradually, you will still feel it when your hands are further apart. That's energy you are feeling. Allow the energy to build while moving your hands farther and farther apart and still feeling the warmth or tingling in your hands. When you are ready, do one of two things: place your hands on any part of your own body you feel needs a boost of energy to stimulate healing, or send the energy away to your pets, nature, trees, or a friend, allowing your intuition to guide you. I recommend training in distant healing if you are drawn to it, and please do not send energy without first asking permission. In your heart and mind, ask, "May I send you this energy?" Wait to hear in your mind and heart a yes or no. It's always better to ask if someone or something wants to receive what you want to give.

★ ★ ★

There are so many things we can do to support relaxation. Use your imagination to develop quick relaxation techniques. Take a walk outdoors, jump up and down, get in your car, or laugh out loud to exercise and relax your stomach muscles. There is no wrong or right way to relax. The important thing is to give the body a message that says, "It is now time to relax," and then the reinforcement to do so. Happy relaxing!

CHAPTER 2

Using Meditation as a Tool for Change

I begin this chapter with both why meditation is so important to our lives and how long meditation has been important to humankind. In the fifth century BCE a Sanskrit document was recorded, called the *Katha Upanishad*. Sanskrit is the Indo-Aryan language of one of the first civilizations known on earth, located in the northwestern region of the India subcontinent. The teachings from oral traditions were put into writing between 1500 and 500 BCE. These writings are so eloquent, and so ancient, that they give perspective to this chapter that my words alone cannot do. We'll begin with four verses from *Katha Upanishad*, part 2, in their entirety. They will tell us why to meditate. And then we'll follow with seven verses from the Upanishads, part 1, that tell us how.

Knowing the senses to be separate
From the Self, and the sense experience
To be fleeting, the wise grieve no more.

Above the senses is the mind,
Above the mind is the intellect,
Above that is the ego, and above the ego
Is the unmanifested Cause.

When the five senses are stilled, when the mind
Is stilled, when the intellect is stilled,
That is called the highest state by the wise.

Meditation enables them to go
Deeper and deeper into consciousness,
From the world of words to the world of thoughts,
Then beyond thoughts to wisdom in the Self.[10]

We meditate because we want to change something in our lives and all our other strategies haven't worked. Being angry just brings on more attack. Being worried just brings on more worry. Working hard just brings on hard work. At some point we become exhausted trying to fight what seems beyond our control. We can't control the weather. We can't control another person. But we can control ourselves. In fact, we are the only thing in our lives that we can control and change. To learn how requires learning who we really are inside. That exploration has gone on as long as humankind has existed.

Let's continue our exploration with another selection from the *Katha Upanishad*. This section tells us why meditation is a tool for change and describes how to meditate as well. I've selected seven verses from part 1 of the *Katha Upanishad* for discussion.

Know the Self as the lord of the chariot and the body as … the chariot[;]
know the intellect as the charioteer and the mind as … the reins.[11]

The passage says that our bodies are vehicles or chariots in this life. The intellect is the operator of our bodies, and the mind is the reins, which respond

10. Eknath Easwaran, trans., *Katha Upanishad*, Veda wikisite, accessed January 30, 2022, 1.3.6, 1.3.7, 1.3.10, and 1.3.13, http://veda.wikidot.com/katha-upanishad-eknath.
11. S. Radhakrishna, trans., "Katha Upanishad," *Principal Upanishads*, Himalayan Academy, accessed January 10, 2022, 1.3.3. https://www.himalayanacademy.com/saivite-scriptures/principal-upanishads/#katha-upanishad.

to the commands of the intellect. The passage asks us to know that we, ourselves, are the lord or owner of the chariot. We are owners of our life experiences. In meditation we begin to feel that there is more to us than how our bodies feel and what our minds think.

The senses … are the horses; the objects of sense the paths …;
the self associated with the body, the senses and the mind … [12]

Next, our senses are viewed as the horses that pull the chariot. That makes sense! In life we are guided by our senses: we jump at a loud bang and stop and view a beautiful sunset. The environment, objects of sense, are the paths we follow. The passage goes on to say that the small self enjoys the life of the body, senses, and mind. But what happens when life is not perfect?

He who has no understanding, whose mind is always unrestrained,
his senses are out of control, as wicked horses are for a charioteer. [13]

Now comes the punch line. If our mind is always unrestrained, then we can no longer control our senses, and our lives are out of control like wicked horses. Meditation literature refers to this as "monkey brain." We think about something, then about something else, then we replay the past, then jump to the future, all the while stimulating the adrenal fight-or-flight system and living with constant stress. The solution is in the next verse!

He … who has understanding, whose mind is always restrained,
his senses are under control, as good horses are for a charioteer. [14]

Meditation teaches us how to restrain our mind and get our senses under control. When that occurs, we are much more able to live the life that we want, the life of well-being. Meditation then goes further.

He who has the understanding for the driver of the chariot and controls the rein of his mind, he reaches the end of the journey … [15]

....

12. Radhakrishna, trans., "Katha Upanishad," 1.3.4.
13. Radhakrishna, trans., "Katha Upanishad," 1.3.5.
14. Radhakrishna, trans., "Katha Upanishad," 1.3.6.
15. Radhakrishna, trans., "Katha Upanishad," 1.3.9.

Meditation puts us in contact with the driver of the chariot, the self that is able to love and understand, to forgive and forget, to pass through life with grace and ease. As we calm the mind and move into the present moment, we understand that life is too precious to be constantly angry and upset. It is far more desirable to be happy and peaceful.

Beyond the senses are the objects … and beyond the objects is the mind; beyond the mind is the understanding and beyond the understanding is the great self.[16]

Ah, now we go deeper. Through meditation we realize that beyond all that we think and see and feel and taste is a greater self. An Inner Self that we can call on at any time for help and inspiration. We are not alone in the world. We are not our bodies; we are not our senses. We are something more, something deeper, higher, better. This is the Self, experienced through meditation.

Beyond the great self is … the spirit. … The final goal.[17]

And at last, we reach our final goal, to know our true Self. The Self that is beyond the physical and material of this world. The Self that is everlasting. The Self that we really are. Meditation brings us all this and more.

In meditation we take control of the reins, the mind, and stop the horses, the five senses of seeing, hearing, smelling, tasting, and touching, for a moment. We ask the charioteer to stop all outward actions like thinking, seeing, moving, talking, touching, and hearing, and we focus within. This allows the surface mind, which usually takes messages from and sends directions back to the senses and powers to reverse its orientation. When the surface mind is no longer distracted by the external world, the mind calms, our focus is directed inward, and we explore new dimensions of our own being. This results in new perceptions and experiences; new, more holistic ways of understanding; and a release from ordinary self-concerns, anxieties, woes, and habits, allowing other ways of feeling and seeing to develop. It is for this purpose that we meditate. To allow ourselves to experience our lives differently, to make new decisions, to grow and develop in peace and love instead of struggle and want.

....

16. Radhakrishna, trans., "Katha Upanishad," 1.3.10.
17. Radhakrishna, trans., "Katha Upanishad," 1.3.11.

In the West, meditation initially earned a bad reputation. Associated with religion or mysticism, meditation's physical and emotional benefits were often ignored. Today meditation is considered one of the essential survival skills to live in our complex world and remain of good mind, body, and spirit.

The Impact of Meditation

Meditation can impact us in many different ways. Here we'll take a look at the types of instances that this might include. From mind and body to emotion and overall vitality, meditation's reach for potential positive impact is impressive!

Impact on Brain Wave Frequencies

Before examining specific research studies, let us take a brief look at meditation as it alters brain wave frequencies. Hans Berger, inventor of EEG machines, first recorded brain wave frequencies in humans in 1924 and was so skeptical that he did not publish his work until 1929.[18] Frequencies are measured in hertz (Hz). One Hz is one complete wave cycle per second. The brain controls a vast array of bodily functions, and its health is essential to the quality of our lives.

The following is a brief description of the effects of each measured brain wave range on the body-mind system. Brain wave information is becoming more prevalent every day as research continues to discover the attributes of different frequencies.[19] The attainment of specific brain waves during meditation results in specific and numerous physiological and psychological benefits.

Gamma, 32–100 Hz: Gamma waves are reported to be the binding mechanism that integrates data in the brain, like the oil in a car makes the engine run smoothly. Gamma frequencies are considered the key to cognition and are known to disappear under anesthesia. They appear to be associated with higher mental function, problem-solving, self-control, self-awareness, language development, and heightened

....

18. Laura Sanders, "How Hans Berger's Quest for Telepathy Spurred Modern Brain Science," *Science News,* July 6, 2021, https://www.sciencenews.org/article/hans-berger-telepathy -neuroscience-brain-eeg.
19. NeuroSonica, "Brainwave Frequencies & Effects," accessed January 12, 2022, https://www .neurosonica.com/the-science/brainwave-types-frequencies.html; Muse, "A Deep Dive Into Brainwaves: Brainwave Frequencies Explained, June 25, 2018, https://choosemuse.com /blog/a-deep-dive-into-brainwaves-brainwave-frequencies-explain.

consciousness and perception. Decreased gamma activity has reportedly been observed in depression, ADHD, Alzheimer's, and autism. Buddhist monks with extensive training in loving kindness meditation have reportedly shown increased gamma activity.

Beta, 15–38 Hz: Beta frequencies occur during objective, active, rapid, rational thinking.

When in beta, we are on full alert and have awareness of our surroundings in an on-guard manner. The mind thinks rapidly in beta, the muscles ready to spring into action. The basic fight-or-flight stress response arises from a beta brain wave frequency. Also arising from that frequency are muscle spasms, chronic pain, and the inability to relax mentally or physically.

Our busy beta mind is full of thoughts and jumping from one thought to another. This is helpful when brainstorming new ideas, but it also creates anxiousness that prevents sleep.

Mu, 12.5–15 Hz: A Mu wave is associated with flow states of mind. The mind is sharp yet relaxed, able to completely focus on the task at hand, whether that task is physical and athletic or mental and creative. On a really good day we all have experienced flow. We bake the perfect cake or make the perfect presentation to an audience, and it is so easy! We climb the side of a mountain or ride horseback through the woods, and it is all so graceful. Olympic athletes win the gold when their performance is in the flow. Even as I am writing this book, I seek the flow of words and take a break when it's not flowing. I also help the flow a bit by listening to relaxing instrumental music while writing!

Alpha, 8–15 Hz: Alpha frequencies produce a daydreaming state of relaxation and creativity. Alpha waves are associated with the beginnings of inward awareness and intuition. Alpha is the initial state of relaxation attained in stress management and meditation to attain a peaceful state of mind. Alpha waves are associated with reduction in the stress hormone cortisol and increase in serotonin, which in turn moves the body from sympathetic nervous system stress to parasympathetic nervous system calmness. Athletes and performers are trained in attaining alpha prior to events, but you need not be an athlete to benefit from alpha. In today's complex world most of us have overstimulated adrenal glands, ready to jump into action to defend ourselves from something that we just thought of that we need defense from. The relaxation techniques in the previous chapter are all designed to move your brain waves into an alpha state of well-being. In addition, alpha is the pathway into the inner realms of consciousness that we explore in this chapter.

Theta, 4–8 Hz: Theta is the inner doorway to the subconscious, a deeply relaxed state of well-being. Theta waves enhance immune function and release neurochemicals that regulate body rhythms of the heart, blood pressure, and breathing, including vasopressin and catecholamine. Theta is the ground for guided imagery and the free flow of thoughts and feelings, allowing emotional processing and relief of negative programming. Deep theta meditation is associated with right brain intuition and activation of other psychic abilities. Theta is where we dream every night. In theta we find ourselves allowing all thoughts without judging them as good or bad. We set down the mantle of always being right or wrong, of guilt or regret. Life is interesting. We are who we are. Theta brings us closer to into the beautiful, glorious selves that we truly are deep inside. In deep theta meditation our right brain intuition and psychic abilities may be activated.

Delta, 0.5–4 Hz: Delta is a deep, dreamless sleep in which the body has the opportunity to repair and regenerate. In delta, the constant chatter of our subconscious minds vacates long enough for the body's natural healing frequencies to be established. Delta has a calming effect on the limbic system and produces antiaging hormones such as DHEA, melatonin, and human growth hormone, which are underproduced in chronic stress and in aging, leading to a host of diseases that have stress as their foundational cause. Deep meditation takes us into what modern energy technologies refer to as a still point: a place of nothingness in which the mind relaxes and the frequencies governing cells reset back toward normal. It is why sleeping is one of the best treatments for illness.

Impact on Health

Studies have shown positive psychological changes during meditation, including brain wave changes that enhance deep feeling of well-being, stress reduction, decreased anxiety and depression, reduction in physical and psychological pain, improved memory, and increased efficiency.[20]

Physiological effects of meditation include more efficient breathing patterns and oxygen consumption, lowering of heart rate and blood pressure, increase in melatonin and in blood flow to the brain.[21] Meditation has been

·····················

20. Daniela Dentico et al., "Short Meditation Trainings Enhance Non-REM Sleep Low-Frequency Oscillations," *PLoS ONE* 11, no. 2 (2016): e0148961, doi:10.1371/journal.pone .0148961; Albert J. Arias et al., "Systematic Review of the Efficacy of Meditation Techniques as Treatments for Medical Illness," *Journal of Alternate and Complementary Medicine* 12, no. 8 (October 2006): 817–32, doi:10.1089/acm.2006.12.817; Jaimie L. Burns, Randolph M. Lee, and Lauren J. Brown, "Effect of Meditation on Self-Reported Measures of Stress, Anxiety, Depression, and Perfectionism in a College Population," *Journal of College Student Psychotherapy* 25 (2011): 132–44, doi:10.1080/87568225.2011.556947; David W. Orme-Johnson et al., "Neuroimaging of Meditation's Effect on Brain Reactivity to Pain," *Neuroreport* 17, no. 12 (August 2006): 1359–63, doi:10.1097/01.wnr.0000233094.67289.a8; Dharma Singh Khalsa, "Stress, Meditation, and Alzheimer's Disease Prevention: Where the Evidence Stands," *Journal of Alzheimer's Disease* 48, no. 1 (2015): 1–12, doi:10.3233/JAD-142766; James C. Elliott, B. Alan Wallace, and Barry Giesbrecht, "A Week-Long Meditation Retreat Decouples Behavioral Measures of the Alerting and Executive Attention Networks," *Frontiers in Human Neuroscience* 8 (2014): 69, doi:10.3389/fnhum.2014.00069.

21. R. Jevning, R. K. Wallace, and M. Beidebach, "The Physiology of Meditation: A Review; A Wakeful Hypometabolic Integrated Response," *Neuroscience Biobehavioral Review* 16, no. 3 (1992): 415–24, doi:10.1016/s0149-7634(05)80210-6; Robert D. Brook et al., "Beyond Medications and Diet: Alternative Approaches to Lowering Blood Pressure; A Scientific Statement from the American Heart Association," *Hypertension* 61, no. 6 (2013): 1360–83, doi:10.1161 /HYP.0b013e318293645f; Gregory A. Tooley et al., "Acute Increases in Night-time Plasma Melatonin Levels Following a Period of Meditation," *Biological Psychology* 53, no. 1 (2000): 69–78, doi:10.1016/S0301-0511(00)00035-1; Danny J. Wang et al., "Cerebral Blood Flow Changes Associated with Different Meditation Practices and Perceived Depth of Meditation," *Psychiatry Research* 191, no. 1 (2011): 60–7, doi:10.1016/j.pscychresns.2010.09.011.

found beneficial in decreasing the fight-or-flight sympathetic overstimulation, reducing cholesterol, and reducing smoking.[22]

According to WebMD, 43 percent of all adults have experienced adverse health effects from stress, and 75 to 90 percent of all doctor's office visits are for stress-related ailments and complaints.[23] Our physical well-being depends upon a healthy immune system, and meditation directly and indirectly boosts the immune system.[24] Over the years of meditating and teaching people how to meditate, I've made some observations. Meditation increases productivity and releases creative potentials in both work and hobbies. Meditators are less likely to blame themselves and more likely to forgive themselves and others. Meditation helps you feel better immediately and in the long term. It is a wonderful substitution for addictions to food, alcohol, or anything you feel you need right now.

Meditation teaches the mind how to observe before reacting and offers space to decide whether to be irritated and angry or not. When you establish a regular meditation practice, you give your mind and body a space and time to relax and just be, a touchstone for the day, and a place to experience kindness given from yourself to yourself.

Sometimes the feelings of well-being scare people. The "I feel so good that something bad is about to happen" people. That is a learned belief—that if you feel good, just wait for the other shoe to drop, or that you don't feel worthy of feeling peaceful and well. All these are feelings that will decrease the longer you meditate. Meditation helps us realize that it is okay to feel good and it is okay to be well, despite what we have learned in the past of experiences from other people. Meditation may also require altering of certain medications, so let your

....

22. Sirawit Bantornwan et al., "Role of Meditation in Reducing Sympathetic Hyperactivity and Improving Quality of Life in Lupus Nephritis Patients with Chronic Kidney Disease," *Journal of the Medical Association of Thailand* 97, suppl. 3 (2014): S101–7, https://pubmed.ncbi.nlm .nih.gov/24772586/; Rashmi Vyas and Nirupama Dikshit, "Effect of Meditation on Respiratory System, Cardiovascular System and Lipid Profile," *Indian Journal of Physiology and Pharmacology* 46, no. 4 (2002): 487–91, https://pubmed.ncbi.nlm.nih.gov/12683226/; Laura Carim-Todd, Suzanne H. Mitchel, and Barry S. Oken, "Mind-Body Practices: An alternative, Drug-Free Treatment for Smoking Cessation?; A Systematic Review of the Literature," *Drug and Alcohol Dependence* 132, no. 3 (October 2013): 399–410, doi:10.1016/j.drugalcdep.2013.04.014.
23. Smitha Bhandari, ed., "The Effects of Stress on Your Body," WebMD, December 8, 2021, https://www.webmd.com/balance/stress-management/effects-of-stress-on-your-body.
24. Tonya L. Jacobs, et al., "Intensive Meditation Training, Immune Cell Telomerase Activity, and Psychological Mediators," *Psychoneuroendocrinology* 36, no. 5 (June 2011): 664–81, doi:10.1016/j.psyneuen.2010.09.010.

doctor know when you have begun a regular meditation practice. For example, the dose of your blood pressure medication may need to be decreased when you become more peaceful inside. You and your doctor will decide when or if changes are necessary. After you establish a regular meditation practice, you may not enjoy sitting around with your friends and being angry over politics or the behavior of coworkers, or the negative energy we spend blaming someone or something else for our condition in life. The practice of meditation leads us into self-responsibility and from there into self-empowerment. Ready for the grand adventure? Let's begin now.

Traditional Meditation Posture and Five Ways to Begin to Meditate

Soon we'll explore foundational theories and practices of the three major forms of meditation. For now, here is guidance for traditional meditation posture that you can follow if you're interested in trying a sitting meditation. Following that summary, you'll find five ways you can begin your meditation practice. Select one and begin with it. Perform it daily for five minutes and experience the results for yourself.

Practice
Traditional Meditation Posture

The traditional posture for meditation is as follows and may be used for all forms of meditation.

1. Sitting with legs crossed, pelvis elevated on a pillow, or sitting in a chair with feet flat on the floor.

2. Hands resting on knees, palms up or palms down.

3. Spine balanced without being rigid.

4. Chin slightly tucked.

5. Eyes gazing downward or closed or gazing slightly up.

6. Mouth slightly open with jaw relaxed.

7. Tip of tongue touching palate ridge just behind upper teeth.

By following this posture, a stillness is induced within the body, making the quieting of the mind easier. Don't feel required to follow this posture as you're starting out if you don't want to. Just know that it's an option. I have mentioned these practices before. The difference is I want you to assume a posture—traditional, sitting in chair, or lying in bed—and hold that posture for five minutes. Set a timer. Do not let the body distract you by moving for five minutes. As close as possible, feel the experience without mental commentary. That is the beginning of meditation!

Practice
Breathing for Five Minutes

Breathe in for a mental count of four, hold for four, breathe out for four, and hold for four. This is a technique you can do anywhere, anytime, to relax.

Practice
Mindfulness for Five Minutes

Feel your breath as it comes in through your nose and goes out through your nose. Stay with the breath. Note each thought you have and imagine it in a bubble of air, floating to the surface and breaking free. Observe the thought bubble and let it go.

Practice
Listen to Music for Five Minutes

Listen to music that relaxes you—really listen, with eyes closed and sitting in a comfortable position. Do not do anything while listening, just be with the music. As you consider what music to listen to, you might keep the frequency in mind and search out specific types of vibration. For example, in the eleventh century, Guido D'Arezzo, a Benedictine monk, created a musical scale that was used in hymns and chants.[25] These tones became lost over the centuries as the Western musical scale evolved. In the mid-1970s Dr. Joseph Puleo, pseudonym Dr. Joseph Barber, a leading herbalist in America, found D'Arezzo's six electromagnetic sound frequencies in the Benedictine hymn for John the Baptist. These frequencies are the Solfeggio scale of music. They begin at 8 Hz (alpha brain wave, Schumann Earth resonance) and progress octave by octave until middle C is vibrating at 256 Hz and A is vibrating at 432 Hz. Tuning music to harmonize with these frequencies is known as scientific tuning. Magical, mystical, scientific healing events can occur when the body and mind come into resonance with the Schumann frequency and its progression through solfeggio. Look for music based on these frequencies.

25. Gaia Staff, "Healing Frequencies of the Ancient Solfeggio Scale," Gaia, March 14, 2022, https://www.gaia.com/article/healing-frequencies-of-the-ancient-solfeggio-scale.

Practice
Visualization for Five Minutes

Visualize the positive and the relaxing. During a quiet time, close your eyes and imagine you are sitting in a place in nature that is very relaxing for you. It may be a place you have been before, or one only you can imagine being at. Let yourself sense, feel, taste, smell, see, and hear that place. Let your body relax; let your mind relax; let yourself spend some time at peace.

Practice
Affirmation for Five Minutes

Use the information from chapter 1 and create an affirmation. Repeat one over and over as you are going to bed. Try to let a positive affirmation be the last thing you think about at night. Then in the morning, repeat it over and over as you are getting ready for your day. I like to use simple ones, like "I am healthy, healed, and whole," "I am abundant, prosperous, and successful," or "I let the past go and am at peace now."

Overview of Three Main Meditation Techniques

Now that you know *why* meditation is good for you, let us discover *how* to meditate. The best definition I have for meditation is that meditation is a skill or technique that involves the development of inward aspects of consciousness to enhance one's abilities to attain one's life goals. That's right—it is a technique to do better in the world! Without the ability to maintain an inner calm, our ventures in the world become chaotic. In meditation, we go inward to find the Source of Life, we bathe in that Source, we renew in that Source, and then we return to the world to do good.

A daily practice of meditation enables us to bring love, peace, joy, and all the other positive attributes into our lives and the lives of those around us. We can only give to others what we have inside ourselves. In meditation, we learn that inside is peace and love. And that is what we then can give to our families, our work, our community, and our world. Powerful stuff!

For clarity, I have divided all meditation techniques into one of three categories or types of meditation: concentration, contemplation, and mindfulness. These are arbitrary divisions, useful in exploring each general type in depth.

Concentration Meditation

Concentration meditation includes forms of meditation that require concentration on a single object or concept. In this form, we focus our undivided attention on something to the exclusion of all other things in our world. This requires the highest mental concentration and involves the calming of all mental processes. To practice concentration meditation, we maintain an increasing concentrated focus of attention on a single object. In doing so, we attain temporary different frequencies of consciousness: alpha, gamma, theta, and delta brain waves.

We all go into different brain wave frequencies daily. Our normal brain wave patterns range from beta when we are active and thinking and reacting to the world around us, to alpha when we begin to relax, back up to beta when we are stimulated, and down to alpha again when we begin to go to sleep at night. During sleep, we alternate between alpha and theta, with occasional trips to delta. In meditation, we learn to control or direct these frequencies to a certain extent. Instead of them just happening to us, we choose to go to alpha, and we do so. The issue is not whether we go into these states; it is that we journey there when we desire to!

Practice
Introduction to Concentration Meditation

Continue with your five-minute practice and try some or all of these, one at a time. If you wish, set your timer for even longer, maybe ten minutes.

Concentrate on an Image

Focus on a candle, a painting, a sunset, a tree, a crystal. The focus is exclusively on the image. Just sit and focus. When thoughts distract the mind, return to the focus. Continually returning to the focus until you are there!

Where is *there*? Our normal consciousness, what we call thinking, involves an awareness of dualism. Something is that, but not this. In meditation, we are able to go beyond this dualism into pure awareness. Philosophers call this space the void, the no-thing. Nondualistic awareness attained during meditation is a space of no conflicts because there are no opposites. This special space of being fills us with peace. We live in a world of black and white, this or that. Meditation takes us into a world of just being. And out of that world our being becomes well again.

Concentrate on a Sound

Focus your attention on the sound of waves breaking on the sand, of a babbling brook, of the pure chant of the universal sound of OM. If you are not into OMing it, try this practice. Sit by yourself or invite a friend to join you. Now sing the vowels! Sing "Aaaaaaaa" three times, putting your soul into the sound. The tone doesn't matter at this point, just sing. Now sing "Eeeeeeee" three times. Then "Iiiiiiii" three times, "Ooooooooo" three times, and "Uuuuuuuu" three times. Notice how you felt before you began to sing and how you feel after. Pick your favorite vowel sound and sing it for five minutes, then for ten minutes. You are meditating!

Concentrate on an Idea

Repeat the word *love, peace, joy,* or *health* over and over. Say it out loud. Say it silently. Repeat it until you go past its concept and discover its feeling and meaning.

Concentrate on a Precept

The traditional form of concentration meditation is the mantra. A mantra is a vehicle for transporting the mind beyond thought. We explore the wonderful world of mantras later in this chapter.

Concentrate on a Sensation

If sitting outdoors, focus on the feeling of the wind on your cheek. Or focus on the breath as it comes in and out through your nose. Later in this chapter we will explore this technique more.

Contemplation Meditation

Contemplation meditation includes forms of meditation that require concentration on a variety of concepts, selecting some and excluding others. This is broader than concentration meditation, yet there is an inward focus to the exclusion of outward stimuli. It involves development of access concentration through a selected concentration meditation technique and the creation of thoughts or images within the mind. Attention is focused upon an image, feeling, or thought to the exclusion of all other stimuli, and results in a change experienced in the outer, objective world because of our inner, subjective experiences.

Practice
Introduction to Contemplation Meditation

Here are some examples of contemplation meditation for you to enjoy and explore further!

Affirmations

We are affirming all the time. We affirm that we don't like this or that. We affirm that we feel tired, or stressed, or ill. Contemplation meditation allows us to change the negatives we affirm into positives, and then, as if by magic, we begin to have a more positive outlook on your lives and our lives change for the better. We worked with affirmations earlier in this book. Pick an affirmation and repeat it throughout the day. It may be as grand as "I am now open to receive the abundance of the universe" or as little as one of my favorites, "I will not scare myself today." Louise Hay wrote the classic book on affirmations called *You Can Heal Your Life*, which you may find helpful.

Visualization and Guided Imagery

Often called self-hypnosis, imagery is used to effect change in the outer world. Athletes use imagery to mentally rehearse performance for greater results. Healing imagery can stimulate the body's response to stress, pain, and disease. Shakti Gawain wrote classic book called *Creative Visualization*. It describes many visualizations and affirmations useful in allowing the mind to help the body heal, from the common cold to more serious diseases. Search YouTube with the keyword *affirmations*. We will explore specific techniques for visualization later in this chapter.

Prayer

Prayer is the oldest form of contemplation meditation. Simple, sincere prayer to your Source works wonders. Prayer is a potent form of meditation and can be practiced anytime, anywhere.

Koan

Koan meditation originates in Japan. A koan is a riddle that must be contemplated upon until the answer reveals itself. A common koan is "What is the sound of one hand clapping?" The answer comes not from our dualistic mind, but from our deeper mind. Years may be spent in koan contemplation. My favorite koan is "What did you look like before your parents were born?" Trying to answer this question sends the mind spinning back and back until, exhausted, it gives up and access to the Higher Self is provided.

Inquiry

Inquiry is another form of potent contemplation meditation. In inquiry, you sit and relax and then begin to ask yourself, "Who am I?" Accept any answers that come but do not dwell on them. Then repeat the question, "Who am I?" Again, wait for the answers to come, and then repeat the question. Eventually, if you stick with it, you will enter an area of truth and wisdom deep within yourself.

Mindfulness Meditation

Mindfulness meditation includes forms of meditation that require non-attached awareness of all thoughts, sensations, and feelings. Nothing is excluded from your awareness. The emphasis is on the observation, without judgment of all phenomena, and the development of access concentration through a selected concentration meditation technique. In insight meditation we observe the contents of our minds and the senses of our body without attachment to anything we observe. This involves a complete, direct, and immediate awareness of everything that presents itself during the meditation experience and results in enduring change through the realization of subject/object dualism and the impermanence of all phenomena.

Let's unpack that last powerful sentence. Enduring change is what I want. I want to change a habit, a health issue, or a negative emotion not only for the time I'm meditating, but for all the times I'm out in the world. Realization of subject/object dualism means that I understand in my outer world things come in black and white and gray. There is a yin for my yang. There is light and dark. And sometimes I get upset when I'm in the dark, when things are not going well in my life. So here comes the third gift of meditation. I realize deep in my soul that nothing is permanent. All things change. Sometimes they change for the good, sometimes they change for the bad. But throughout all change, I remain deep within me safe and healed and whole. And when I touch this deep place within me, I can accept change with a touch of grace. I needn't be so frightened by it. I can sit and breathe and do what is necessary without falling apart on the outside because I have touched the place on my inside that never falls apart. That is always there for me. That is the home I will return to after the use of this body and brain are ended. Meditation allows us access to the peace that passeth all understanding, the peace that is not concerned with how dualistic and impermanent this world is, because *I am*.

During mindfulness meditation, you don't think about, don't analyze, and don't intellectualize. Instead, you experience the flow of thoughts and sensations. You learn how to go with the flow, not against it, and to use a light touch and trust the process as you move toward well-being.

Practice
Introduction to Mindfulness Meditation

Are you ready to go a bit further and spend ten minutes on one of these mindfulness practices today?

Awareness of Breath
Become aware of your breath as it comes and goes through your nose. You may choose to simply count each breath, not trying to influence it, but simply observing and counting.

Awareness of Thought
Become aware of your thoughts. Quietly observe each thought that passes through your mind and label it as past or future. It will be one or the other, because if you are truly centered in the present moment, you will have no thoughts to label!

Awareness of Sensation
Become aware of sensations by observing them within the experience of meditation.

Awareness of Feeling
Become aware of feelings by going beyond the feeling to experience the space and energy within.

In the following sections we will explore each technique in depth. For now, happy meditating!

The Practice of Mindfulness

Stop a moment before reading on. What is on your mind right now? Are you wondering what the topic of mindfulness practice is all about? Are you thinking about what you are going to do next? Or are you thinking about what you just did?

Our minds contain thousands and thousands of thoughts each day. And each thought has a direct impact on our emotions and on our bodies. Rarely do we experience the present moment. We are locked in the past or planning the future. When was the last time you were truly mindful of the moment? The usual answer is "When I was on vacation, and I saw a beautiful sunset. I was just there!" It is possible to be on vacation every day. The skill involved is the practice of mindfulness.

In mindfulness, we observe inward, watching our thoughts without attachment to them, similar to lying on the grass and watching the clouds go by. This art of nonattachment to our thoughts results in great healing, peace, and insight. Author and researcher Jon Kabat-Zinn has demonstrated that simply by being mindful of physical and mental pain, we can overcome—or rather, come through—and experience peace.[26] In the practice of mindfulness, we become less judgmental, more able to observe ourselves acting rather than being the actor, have more patience and willingness to look upon things with a fresh mind. There is less striving and more letting go and allowing with continued practice.

Our thoughts are like unruly children, constantly pulling us here and there. And this constant pulling is the source of our stress and pain. Mindfulness is the skill that allows us to watch our thoughts and feelings without being pulled by them. Initially, in practice all this mental chatter preoccupies us. Then we begin to realize that we do have control. By noticing and observing, we stop reacting. And it is our reactions to our thoughts that can bring us emotional stress and physical disease.

....

26. Jon Kabat-Zinn, *Full Catastrophe Living: Using the Wisdom of Your Body and Mind to Face Stress, Pain, and Illness*, rev. ed. (New York: Random House, 2013).

Practice
Basic Mindfulness Meditation

The practice is quite simple. To begin, set your timer or stopwatch for five minutes. Then sit in a comfortable position, close your eyes, and focus on your breath. *Feel* the breath coming and going, going and coming, through your nose. Your breath becomes the vehicle to carry you toward peace.

Now notice how easily you become distracted from the feel of your breath. A thought travels through your mind. That thought leads to another, and another. Finally, you remember that you are supposed to be feeling your breath, and you return. But from where did you return? Where does the mind go?

Experiment again and this time you feel a pressure or pain in your body. You follow that pain and another series of thoughts results. And again, you return to the breath. Each time you return to the sensation of your own breath on your nose, you have gained a little more control over your own mind. You are learning to not let your mind carry you away!

When you are ready, lengthen your five-minute practice to ten minutes, twenty minutes, or more. Experiencing longer practice periods will allow you to enter a space beyond your thoughts. Direct experience of this still space beyond thought can have a transformative and profoundly healing effect on body, emotion, mind, and life. For me, it feels like slipping through a film or membrane. Suddenly the brain is quiet, the body is quiet. There is a sense of expansive peace. Meditation brings us brief glimpses, because once we reach it, our minds say, "Oh great, we're there," and thoughts then push us out. So are you ready? Set aside at least five minutes every day to sit and feel your breath. Enjoy your practice!

Deepening the Practice of Mindfulness

Earlier in this book we looked at the *Katha Upanishad* and how the verses describe the process of the meditation from 500 BCE. The owner of the chariot is the expansive Self, the driver the small and restricted self, the chariot our body, the reins our mind, the horses our senses, and the environment their path.

A more modern analogy is that of getting into a taxicab and telling the driver that we want to go north. A second later we tell the driver we wish to go south. A second after that we decide to go west. Then east. Steady control is required to guide our experience mechanisms, be they taxicabs or chariots, through life. Most of us spend most of our days out of control! We have so many thoughts that send us into the past or into the future and take away our present moment of power. Mindfulness meditation allows us to contact the present and empowers us to creative action.

Keeping with the taxi analogy, we identify with the taxicab, the steering wheel, and the road and forget that we are paying for the ride and can direct the cab where we please. In the practice of mindfulness we observe our thoughts, sensations, and feelings without becoming attached to them. We assert control by letting go of all the surface clutter and by realizing that all these things going on are not us.

In the book *A Gradual Awakening* Stephen Levine uses the metaphor of a train to describe thoughts and thinking.[27] Imagine standing on the roadside, watching a train go by. Each boxcar on the train contains a thought. In one boxcar there is the thought about the rent due next week. In another is a thought about what you are going to have for dinner tonight. The goal of the practice of mindfulness is to see the landscape beyond the train. We begin to meditate. We focus on our breath, coming and going. We feel the breath at the nostrils. We begin to see the landscape. Then suddenly a boxcar thought goes by. In this boxcar we are arguing with our partner. We hop aboard that boxcar and we are off and down the track. One thought leads to another, and to another. We are far and away from following our breath, from seeing the landscape, until we remember to return again to our breath.

....

27. Stephen Levine, *A Gradual Awakening* (New York: Anchor Books, 1989), 29–31.

Practice
Working Through Distraction in Mindfulness Meditation

Begin by finding a comfortable place where you will not be disturbed. One student of mine put a big pillow in the bathroom and meditated there. It was the only place in the house where she had any privacy! Set a timer for twenty minutes or more, then set it away from you so you will not be tempted to peek to see how much time is left. Close your eyes and focus on your breath. Feel the breath coming and going, going and coming from your nose. Simply observe your breathing. Do not try to control it. When you find yourself distracted from the breath, you may try the following.

Distracted by Thoughts or Feelings
Try labeling each thought and feeling. Use such labels as "future thought," "past thought," "angry feeling," and "loving feeling." As soon as you have labeled the thought, return immediately to the sensation of your breath.

Distracted by Sensations
Avoid the tendency to respond to sensations. Do not scratch an itch or adjust position because of a discomfort. Notice the itch as itch and the discomfort as pain. And return immediately to the sensation of your breath. The mind cannot calm down if the body is in constant motion. If you are really in an awkward position, then mindfully change that position and return to your breath.

Over a period of time, with consistent daily practice, you will naturally become less responsive to and more responsible for the contents of your mind. Consistent practice is essential. You cannot learn how to drive if you only get in behind the wheel once a month for twenty minutes. Meditation is a skill and a habit. Once you have developed both, you will not want to be without them. There are some added benefits. Try extending your practice time to forty minutes or even one hour once a week. You may find yourself traveling to the landscape completely beyond thought—a wonderful place of pure healing, light, and love. But do not expect it! An expectation is just a thought. And thoughts keep us from experiencing the light of pure awareness. Meditation allows us to experience that we are more than our thoughts. Thoughts are just encapsulated energy. The experience of Essential Self, our state of pure energy, will heal and free us to grow and love and be well.

Mantra Meditation as a Form of Concentration

We were introduced to concentration meditation earlier in the chapter already, but here we are going to focus on one specific version to deepen our practice.

The first concentration meditation was experienced as cave men and women stared into their fire at night. I once heard that while prayer is talking to God, meditation is listening. Unfortunately, confusion occurs when meditation is associated with religion. A form of meditation is used in all religions, just as candles are burned in many religions. However, you do not have to be in a church to burn a candle. You do not have to follow a particular spiritual path to practice meditation. From Jesuit priests to Tibetan Buddhists, from the chants of India to the songs of Native Americans, meditation has been with us for centuries. One form of meditation, concentration, was popularized in the West in the form of mantra used by Maharishi Mahesh Yogi in the 1960s and trademarked as Transcendental Meditation (TM). Attention from the medical community came in the 1970s through Herbert Benson, MD. Dr. Benson studied the techniques of TM and westernized them into a formula of practice for inducing the "relaxation response."[28] Both TM and the relaxation response use a form of meditation called mantra to focus the mind. Mantras are what we are focusing on here.

A mantra, or specific sound, is used as a vehicle for the mind to ride upon to attain deeper states of concentration and being. In Transcendental Meditation, the sound mantra is selected by the instructor to vibrate with the student in a special way. Mantras usually have no meaning to the meditator, but the sound quality is conducive to producing deep rest and refined awareness.

....

28. Herbert Benson and Miriam Z. Klipper, *The Relaxation Response* (New York: Avon Books, 1976).

Try the following sounds out loud and experiment with the note and rhythm to find the best tones for your healing and well-being. Examples of sounds:

- OM, AUM, AMEN, AMIN, and HUM are the universal sound of awareness.
- AH-OU-MM uses a three-part breath to expand the sound.
- HU is the sound of love, balance, and harmony.
- AH is the sound of emotion, desire, and creativity.
- EH (EE) is the sound of soul force and universal life.

When the sound is sung out loud, the combined effect of the deep breathing required to produce the sound and the tonal qualities of the sound itself produces frequencies for profound relaxation. The sound may also be repeated silently, in harmony with the breath to focus the mind.

Toning is the practice of sounding to specific frequencies for specific benefits. Use the keywords *vocal toning* on YouTube and tone along. We discussed the Solfeggio frequencies earlier. Sounding tuning forks of various frequencies, then toning along to them is another healing practice.

Mantras can be as complex and sacred, or as simple and joyous as you wish. The first mantra I heard was long ago on a Moody Blues album, *In Search of the Lost Chord*. On one song, simply called "OM," they sang "Aaaa aaaa ummmm," over and over. I was entranced. And this was long before I had ever heard of meditation. Years ago, my husband and I studied with an Indian swami, a type of guru or holy man, who gave us a personal mantra. Another time, a Sufi holy man instructed me in a healing mantra. I use all at different times, depending on my intuition to guide me to what would be most beneficial at the time.

The most important point is to find a sound or phrase that feels good to you. When you say it out loud or silently, allow a feeling of peace and surrender and protection to come to you. And then use it!

Practice singing the sound or phrase out loud, alone or with others. Repeat it silently while meditating or just before going to sleep at night. Find the time to go within and you will be truly amazed at the results! OOOOOMMMMM.

Practice
Mantra Meditation

In this practice we will concentrate on a word or phrase.

General Procedure

The following general procedure may be followed during this form of meditation. Select a word or phrase that reflects your belief system; a line from a prayer; a concept such as love, peace, or joy; an affirmation; or an image of peace.

1. Find a comfortable position and close your eyes.

2. Relax your muscles from feet to head.

3. Be aware of your breathing and begin to repeat the word or phrase silently or out loud.

4. Maintain a passive attitude and continue for a set period of time, usually ten to twenty minutes.

5. Practice the technique at least five minutes each day.

Traditional Mantras

If you aren't sure what to use as your mantra and you would like to meditate using traditional mantras, here are some that you can try working with:

- "Gate gate paragate, parasamgate, bodhi, svaha" (gah-tay, gah-tay, pah-r-gah-tay, pah-r-sum-gah-tay boh-dee swah-hah). Sanskrit for "Beyond, beyond, the great beyond, beyond that beyond, to thee homage."

- "OM Namaha Shivaya" (OM, na-mah, shee-vah-yaa). Sanskrit for "I honor the God/Goddess within."

- "Aum mani padme hum" (ah-owm mah-nay paud-may hoom). Tibetan meaning "The All is a precious jewel in the lotus flower that blooms in my heart."

- "Ananda maya moksha" (ah-nan-da, my-ah, mook-sha). *Ananda* is bliss or joy, *maya* is illusion or fear, and *moksha* is liberation. This mantra is used to liberate us from fear and move us into joy in body, mind, and spirit.

- "Hail Mary, full of grace..."—a Christian prayer.

- "Our Father, who art in heaven..." or any line from the Lord's Prayer.

- "Not my will but thine be done..." or any meaningful spiritual phrase.

Modern Mantras

If the traditional mantras don't feel right to you, trying constructing your own! You can make your own mantra by creating a six-to-ten-syllable phrase that is personally meaningful and repeated effortlessly in rhythm with the breath. Here are some examples:

- The waves roll in and roll out.

- Returning to my center.

- River flowing into the sea.

- Peace is with me now.

- I'm willing to change and grow.

- I relax, I release, I let go.

- I am loved, loving, and loveable.

Visualization and Guided Imagery

Visualization and guided imagery are both forms of our own imagination. We tell ourselves a story or hear a story and apply it to our own lives. Because what we see is so closely connected to our physical body, visualization can be used to develop skills from Olympic performances to winning golf strokes. We have to be able to see something in our mind's eye before we can perform it. Even something as simple as picking up a spoon requires this mental imagery. In addition, our bodies accept as real our emotions. If we visualize being afraid on a roller coaster, our wonderful little adrenals will start to secrete their stress hormones, and all of a sudden, our heart rate increases, our breathing quickens, and we are in physiological fight-or-flight response. The same thing occurs when we watch a scary movie. That's how powerful visualizing is. Guided imagery is simply having someone else guide you in what you are experiencing with your eyes closed.

Visualization

Visualization is the process we use to form a mental picture of the world. This seeing with the mind's eye may involve actual seeing, imagining, pretending, feeling, knowing, or sensing—the mode differs with each person. To discover your mode of visualizing, close your eyes after reading this sentence and visualize a pink elephant.

When you open your eyes, answer this question: What direction was the elephant facing?

How you were able to determine the direction of the elephant is your current mode of visualizing. Some people clearly see the elephant in their minds. Others simply know which direction the elephant was facing. It is like reading a book. How do you picture the characters? Would you recognize them on the street? There is no wrong or right way to visualize. Just do it and accept your mode as correct for you.

Guided Imagery

Guided imagery is a technique used by oneself or another to direct visualization in specific ways by describing a scene that you imagine, visualize, as clearly as you can. Examples of scenes are a mountain setting, images of the self as a successful person, or pictures of what an emotion may look like.

Guided imagery may be used to foster empathy, set goals, enhance creativity, manage stress, rehearse the future, practice a skill, improve performance, relieve pain or fear, control habits, promote personal growth, enhance learning, and promote healing. Other purposes of guided imagery and visualization include discovering or changing subconscious programs, mentally practicing motor skills and performances, relaxing and transforming reactions into responses, connecting with others, and connecting with one's Higher, Inner, or Deeper Self.

Practice
Create a Special Place Using Guided Imagery

The following is a guided imagery you may practice. Read the imagery into a recording device or app and listen to it or have a friend read it to you. This imagery contains all the steps to using imagery for healing and well-being.

In this practice you will first go through a relaxation experience. Following that, you will mentally create a safe place in nature that you can return to each time you use the visualization. You will be guided to include a dwelling to decorate and a screen or window on which to view your images. During this practice, you will use a combination of projective and receptive techniques. With projective techniques you are consciously creating the scenes before you. With receptive techniques you are open to receive images from the subconscious and supraconscious mind. The practice will conclude with an energizing experience or imagery. For best results, read the imagery slowly to another person, with pauses between sentences, or record it in your own voice on your smartphone or computer to listen to.

A Basic Guided Imagery Script

Begin by taking a deep breath, in through the bottoms of your feet and out through the top of your head. Take a second breath, in through your feet and out through your head. And a third breath.

Imagine, pretend, or feel that there is a ball of light about six inches above the top of your head. It is a ball of warm light. You can see it as a white light, or you may even see it as a different color. It is about six inches above the top of your head, and in a moment, you will be bringing that light into your head to relax your body. Feel the light now coming into the top of your head and entering into your forehead. Your forehead and scalp relax as the light touches them. The back of your head relaxes, almost as if where the light touches, an internal massage and internal balancing is occurring. The light caresses the cells and tissues in your face, and you watch yourself relax with the light.

You feel the light now flowing down into your eyes and eyelids. Your eyeballs feel as if they are relaxing, being massaged. The temples and back of your head are relaxing. Light goes down now into your cheeks, and your jaws relax. Your ears are warm and relaxed. The back of your head is warm and relaxed. Feel the relaxation occurring, feel the balancing occurring. The light now flows down your throat and the back of your neck. Your throat relaxes. You may wish to swallow. Swallowing will only take you deeper into relaxation.

Allow the light now to flow across the tops of your shoulders, giving an internal massage to the muscles that are on the tops of your shoulders, and you are feeling and relaxing even more. Feel the warmth of circulation, growing relaxation. The light flows now down your arms to your elbows, forearms, wrist, hands, and fingers. As this warmth, this light, this relaxation flows, you may even feel a slight tingling in your fingertips. Allow your arms to relax. Allow the cells and tissues to relax.

The light now flows to the base of your throat, then it begins to expand through your chest and upper back. Each place the light touches becomes more balanced, more whole, more healed. The light expands throughout your chest and breasts, heart, and lungs. Allow the light to flow now into your lower back and surround your kidneys, flowing down into your stomach, intestines, and pelvic area. Each place the light touches becomes more balanced and more healed. Light now flows into your pelvic area, massaging and relaxing, back and front. Cells, tissues, and organs function perfectly now. Relax.

The light flows further down the thighs and knees. Deeper and deeper into relaxation. Flowing down into the ankles and feet. Wonderfully relaxed. Take a moment and send this light to any place in your body that still feels a bit tense. Use your mind, your imagination to send the light to any place of tension. Simply by shining the light, notice the release from the tension. Allow the light to flow out through the pores of your skin, surrounding you in a halo, a cocoon of light. A peaceful cocoon of light, just the right temperature. Feel the light.

Notice that from this cocoon of light a small bubble of light emerges. Place a portion of your consciousness into this bubble and feel it begin to float up. This bubble is going to be your vehicle for travel into your own mind. As part of you floats up in this bubble of light, you may even be able to look down upon yourself and see yourself from above. An unusual view!

Let this bubble of light rise up and begin to travel, taking you and your mind to a place that represents peace and beauty and safety for you. Feel yourself traveling now, across the land. Maybe heading toward the beach, or the mountains, or the river, or the desert. Letting yourself travel toward this place of safety, this place of peace, this place of joy. Seeing it now more clearly in your mind, arrive at this place and step out of the bubble.

Look around. What do you see? Look at the sky. What color is it? Are there clouds? What kind of day is it? Are there trees around? What kind of trees? Notice the colors and the textures. What does this place smell like? Is it the saltiness of the ocean, or the deep, earthy scent of the mountains and forest, or the clear, dry scent of the desert? Is there a breeze blowing? What does it feel like on your skin? Reach down and feel what you are standing on.

Run the sand through your fingers, or the leaves, or the grass. Another deep breath and just enjoy being here for a moment. Just enjoy letting yourself experience the feelings of this place.

When you are ready, turn around and look behind you. You will see a structure of some sort. It could be a cabin, or a tree house, or a cave, and so on. Notice the structure. What is it made of? Are there windows in it? Go now with your mind to the front door. Notice what the door is like. Open the door and walk inside. This is your retreat center where your most powerful visualizations will occur.

The first thing you want to do is to decorate the inside in the style that is comfortable to you. Stand in the center of the room now and face the north wall. Facing the north wall of the room, notice what is on it. Is it wood or painted? What color is it? Are there windows on the north wall, or a fireplace, or a computer system? Are there chairs on the north side of the room? Is there carpeting on the floor, or is it wood or some other material? Decorate the north wall any way you wish. You may place a picture on it if you want to or a certain piece of furniture. It is your wall, and you may decorate it any way you want.

When you are ready, turn to the right and face the east wall. Again, notice what is on it and what is near it. Are there windows? Curtains on the windows? Is there a little eating area on the east side? Arrange the east just right for you. When you are ready, turn again and face the south. What is on the south wall? Notice the colors, the textures, the objects in the south of your room. Again, decorate this area, and when you are ready, turn again to face the west wall. Put anything you want to on this wall. Allow images to come, and if they do not, make up your own! Now turn to the center of the room.

In the center of the room is the most comfortable chair you can imagine. It is a chair that you can sit in and feel safe and protected. Notice the color, the texture of your chair. It is a wonderfully cozy chair. Go and sit down in the chair and snuggle in. Let the chair hold and support your body. Feel how wonderful it feels to be relaxing in this special chair.

Notice now that by your fingertips are two buttons, up and down. Press the down button and a screen comes down in front of you: a movie screen, about five to ten feet in front of you. A big, wide, movie screen. This is the screen on which you are going to do your visualizations.

First, we are going to initiate the screen to make it even more real in our minds. As the screen comes down, you notice that next to you in the chair on the floor are a big bucket of red paint and a big housepainter's brush. Take the brush of red paint and paint your name on the screen, letter by letter. See the letters clearly stand out on your own screen. When you finish, sit back in your seat. Now we will do a color test pattern on the screen. Mentally change your name on the screen from red to orange. See your name changing to orange on the screen. Change the orange to yellow. See your name in yellow changing to green. The green now changes to blue. And the blue changes to violet. The violet changes to white now. If your screen is white, and your name is now white, you will see your name fading into the screen. If the screen is black, change your name to black and see it fading into the screen.

On the screen, project this morning. See yourself on the screen waking up this morning. Watch yourself waking up. What did you do first? Go through the entire morning from the time you woke up until you arrived at this place of meditation. See it as vividly as possible without strain or tension. You are developing the ability to visualize!

Place another image on the screen. This time see yourself standing in a meadow, with the forest just beyond it. See yourself standing in that meadow, with the grass blowing in the wind. The sun is out but not too warm. The temperature is just right. And there is a path that winds toward the forest.

At this time, your choice is to sit in your chair and watch yourself walk the path or, if you wish, get out of your chair and step into the screen so that you now see the path from the perspective of you walking on it—from your own eyes. Begin to walk the path, noticing the wildflowers, feeling the gentle wind. You are now at the edge of the woods. Something shiny and smooth attracts your attention on the path, and you reach down to pick it up. You hold it in your hand and look at it. This object is a symbol for you, and the symbol tells you something about how to develop your relaxation and meditation ability. It may not be clear to you at this very moment what the symbol means, but thinking about the symbol during the coming week will assist you in learning to relax and meditate at deeper and deeper levels.

Step back out of the screen, sit down again on the chair, and let the image of the meadow fade on the screen. Let one more image go onto the screen, an image of you interacting with someone in the future. See yourself and the other person having an interaction that will come out in a wonderful way for both of you. Feel the happiness between you. It may be that a problem is resolved so both of you are satisfied. It may be that something has been said that needed to be said. Rehearse the scene. You can either be in the scene or watch the scene from your chair. When the scene is over, once again sit down in your chair. Let the image fade from the screen. Press the up button by your fingertips and see the screen returning to the ceiling.

Stand up from your chair, look around the room, and know that you can come back here anytime you wish. Know that each time you come back the room will become more real for you. You will be able to do more decorating. It will represent to your mind the place of imagination, creativity, and work for the highest good of all concerned. Look once more around the room, and then head toward the door, feeling very good about the room you have created. Step out into the scene of nature and feel again the peace that you have when you are here. You deserve to experience this more and more in your life.

Find the bubble that brought you here and step inside. You feel yourself beginning to return to the present. The bubble comes slowly into the room you occupy in the present. You now feel the bubble separating at the bottom of your feet into many smaller bubbles. These bubbles of light are energizing, vitalizing bubbles of light. When they enter the bottoms of your feet, your feet begin to tingle slightly with this energy, this awakening, this aliveness. As the light moves through your feet and ankles, you begin to move your toes and ankles around, feeling more and more energized as the bubble of light moves up into your calves and knees and thighs. Letting the energy come back in, feeling the aliveness of the energy. The energy is moving now up into your midsection, up to your shoulders and down your arms and hands, feeling more and more energized. Moving down a little bit, beginning to stretch as energy comes up your throat. When it reaches your head and eyes, your eyes open naturally. You wake up, feeling refreshed and renewed, feeling relaxed.

This guided imagery takes you through the sequential steps of any good imagery. First, you relax. Second, you go to a place that is comfortable and beautiful for you. By creating a special house or room to go to, you remind your subconscious that when you are there, work will be done. Each time you return you are able to go into deeper states of meditation. The screen has a special safety feature in this type of meditation. It allows you to step into it when you want to experience your images directly, and out of it when you want to observe rather than become involved. And finally, using the bubble helps you return to your natural state of consciousness in a gentle and easy fashion.

Use your creativity. Play with your visualizations. Make up stories of the perfect future and visualize/experience yourself in the story. The variations are endless and only limited by your imagination. Explore, enjoy, and have fun!

Raising Consciousness with Meditation

Imagine that you live in a seven-story building. In fact, you *own* the building! The building has so many rooms that you have not visited all of them. For most of your life, you have stayed on the ground floor—just to be near the earth. But even on the ground floor, you have not explored all the rooms. Once in a while, you have ventured up to the higher floors. From there you have looked down upon a different world than the one you can see from the ground. From the higher perspective, problems do not look as real, as serious, as they seem from the ground. It seems more peaceful on the higher floors, but you just have so much to do at ground level that you do not have a lot of time to hang around up there. You visit occasionally, then hurry back to ground level.

This is the path of meditation. Meditation does not take you anywhere that you do not already own within your own mind. Meditation allows you to access the different planes and worlds of consciousness within the building of your own mind. Wouldn't it be nice to go anywhere in your building whenever you wish? Wouldn't it be nice to live on a higher floor for a while, and then return to your ground floor with new insights and new resolutions for old problems?

The following is a guide to the building you own. It is offered in hopes that you will want to visit each floor for yourself. All you need do is go inside with your meditation and visit the reality the map is directing you toward!

Ground Floor: The Physical Plane of Consciousness

Most of the world, most of the time, lives here on the physical plane of consciousness. On this plane, the physical body is very real to us. We devote great attention to keeping the body well, to keeping our house clean, to working for physical food and money. Yet even the physical has a component of energy that folks are becoming aware of. We have a physical body, and we also have an etheric or energy body. And both live on this first level, the ground floor.

Our physical body consists of atoms and cells and organs and bones and tissues. Our etheric or energy bodies consist of the frequencies that form the physical body. The energy body and physical body are connected by our minds and emotions. When we feel stress, our physical body reacts. Chronic stress creates chronic disease. We have decorated many rooms on this first floor. We have a room that we lived in as a child. Another room as a young adult. Another as a mate or father or mother. And yet there are still many empty rooms waiting for us to decorate. We "play" games on the first floor. The game of wealth or scarcity. The game of love or loneliness. The game of fear and anxiety or the game of compassion and hope. We have free will to play any game we wish on the first floor. However, meditation advises us to not take any of these games too seriously, because there is much more to our consciousness than one floor.

How do we change rooms on the ground floor, the physical level? We change through meditation by changing our frequencies.

Second Floor: The Emotional Plane of Consciousness

The second floor houses our emotional body. Some refer to it as the astral or psychic plane. This is the first floor of only wave frequency. On the first floor our frequencies were much slower and our waves easily turn into apparently solid particles. On the second floor we can send energy to our first floor as we explore our dreams, our fantasies, our fears, and our nightmares. It is the floor where good fights evil, of angels and demons. In some rooms of this floor ghosts hang around to complete unfinished business before they go higher in their own consciousness.

We visit this second-floor astral plane to observe and release what we find no longer necessary for our highest good. We tap into higher energy frequencies that are helpful to us on the first floor. If we have attained even a small level of mastery in our mindfulness meditation, we move up in frequency and visit for a while. If we know that our thoughts are only thoughts and that we can observe them without becoming involved in them, we can watch the movies that are always playing on the second floor. Many meditation traditions instruct new disciples to completely avoid this floor and go higher. Many psychics visit this floor and gain advice for their clients. Whether the advice is helpful or not depends upon the spiritual development of the psychic. If the psychic knows there is more to spirit than the astral plane and knows how to guide their client beyond to the correct rooms, then the advice is felt by the client as warm and loving. However, if the person with proclaimed psychic abilities has not done their own spiritual homework, the advice is often fear-based, predicting consequences and outcomes or giving the client a list of things that he or she must do.

Treat this second floor of your consciousness at your personal movie theater. Go there in meditation to create beautiful images of your life and access a higher frequency energy for your body. Watch the movies about the past and future with a sense of truly being in a movie theater, knowing that you can leave if the movie doesn't suit you, or watch it until the end if it is giving you good advice and insight.

Third Floor: The Mental Plane of Consciousness

On the third floor you house your causal body, or soul, and your mental body, or personality. Your soul consists of your abstract thoughts and directs you to the lessons you have chosen to learn while residing on the ground floor. These lessons appear the same for all of us and may be divided into four basic categories:

1. *Lessons about Health:* How to use the higher qualities of love, will, and mind to overcome health issues.

2. *Lessons about Wealth:* How to use the higher qualities of love, will, and mind to overcome issues about finances and material abundance.

3. *Lessons about Happiness:* How to use the higher qualities of love, will, and mind to be in relationship in a positive way with ourselves and with others.

4. *Lessons about Purpose:* How to best develop and fulfill your life purpose.

We are all studying these lessons. We are all taking tests on the ground floor arranged by our souls to see if we understand the curriculum that we have developed on the third floor. Just like when we were in school, sometimes the lessons are hard, and we must do a lot of work before we get it. Other times our understanding comes easily, and we enjoy the lessons.

We become aware of our advisers at this third plane of consciousness and experience their ability to assist us. Their view is higher on the third floor, broader, wiser, and gentler. We use our personality, our concrete thoughts, to work through the lessons on the ground floor. We use our soul to guide us from the third floor. Soul guidance for ground floor lessons is always available. We just have to go to the third floor, through meditation, to find it.

Fourth Floor: The Buddhic Plane of Consciousness

As we begin to go higher, the view of the ground begins to change. Imagine looking out a window on the ground floor of a building. Notice the trees, bushes, cars, and people. Now go up three stories and look at the same scene. The image changes. Now you have an ever-broader perspective on your life. You are looking down upon what was once right before you. You have a different view that allows different ways of being to occur on the first floor.

The fourth floor contains the Buddhic notions of spiritual love and spiritual will. This love and will transcend the ground floor, the personal ego ideal of love and will. Love at this level is unconditional and vast. It does not make demands for performance—the idea that I love you if you will. Instead, it is the beginning of understanding that we are made of the same stuff as our creator, that we are love. Will is "thy will be done" and more when looking for the highest outcome to all affairs.

Fifth Floor: The Atmic Plane of Consciousness

The hallmark of this floor is a unification of will. Spiritual now manifests as "Father, my will is one with yours." There is a movement toward ultimate unity that begins on the fifth floor. No longer struggling between personal will and spiritual will, one realizes that there really is no difference. This floor gives direct access to Christ consciousness and knowing that though I did not create myself, I and my Father, Creator, are one.

Beginning on this floor is a transcendence above and beyond words. An inner knowing, without word-images, comes into awareness. The knowing that you will be in the right place at the right time and take the right actions, all without personal effort. This beginning of unity is a truly freeing experience and is often developed in moments of profound meditation.

Sixth Floor: The Monadic Plane of Consciousness

Here is the blending of spiritual will and love with wisdom and active intelligence. Here lies the knowing of oneness.

Once, my husband and I went on a meditative quest for enlightenment. After many twists and turns in our venture, we were able to experience a moment, an eternity of oneness. During our visit to this sixth floor, we discovered that there was no difference between us and anything else. We were one with the trees, the grass, and the sky. There was no point where we ended and the world began. This was a felt experience, not an intellectual one. In that endless moment of eternity, we were the vastness of all we beheld. We were one.

That kind of experience did not happen often to us. Visiting the sixth floor requires diligence, and faith, and trust. It cannot be forced. We cannot barge our way in. But we can learn to relax and allow moments of oneness. We can intend to invite them into our lives through our meditation.

Seventh Floor: Adi Plane of Consciousness

Beyond words, beyond description, beyond thought, beyond feeling. The great beyond that is sometimes called the void or the no-thing. A place of infinite healing as our separated self returns to its Source. As the consciousness in the sunbeam returns to the sun. As a wave returns to the ocean. We return *home*.

Why Visit Other Floors?

The final question is, why bother to visit all the rooms and floors in our house? Why not just live on the ground floor? We visit because somewhere deep inside we know that we are more than flesh and bones. We know that there is something inside calling us to our purpose, our potential. We visit to discover what that purpose and potential are. We visit to receive deep healing and cleansing. We visit to transform our lives from the ordinary to the extraordinary. We visit because the building is ours, all the rooms are ours, and we are called to experience our fullness.

Meditation connects us to our source, whether we refer it as God, Goddess, All That Is, as Inner Wisdom, or simply Source. The house with many floors, the house with many rooms, or mansions are all different levels of awareness and consciousness. If God was the sun, we are all sunbeams. As we journey higher in our frequencies, our vibrations, we approach this sun. Way-showers like Jesus and Buddha and Mohammed, to name a few, vibrated closer to the sun than most. We all have the potential to live our lives higher if we choose.

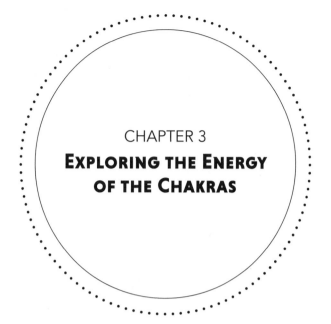

CHAPTER 3

EXPLORING THE ENERGY
OF THE CHAKRAS

The concept of chakras, spinning wheels of energy with definite locations on the etheric or energy body, was first mentioned in the Vedas, texts written in Sanskrit by Indo-Aryan people between 1500 and 500 BCE.[29] They are traditionally an Eastern philosophy and distantly related to the Chinese meridian system first recorded around 100 BCE. Both energy systems have gained attention today as less invasive ways to treat the body and mind. Chakras, places where finer energy infuses matter, contain the keys to our physical, mental, and spiritual well-being. Knowing the relationship between mind-body energy frequencies, chakras, and the physical body is helpful to explain the work that we do while living on the ground floor in the building metaphor we just used. Chakra energy connects the ground floor physical body with the second floor astral or energy body.

....

29. Joshua J. Mark, "The Vedas," World History Encyclopedia, June 9, 2020, https://www
.worldhistory.org/The_Vedas/.

When I was a young, I use to visit my grandparents' house to spend the night in their upstairs bedroom. This was an old home, with a grate-type vent in the floor to allow heat to rise up from the living room into the upstairs bedroom. The vent was over their couch. They would put me to bed, and I would lie on the floor upstairs to watch them through the vent and listen to them talk. Sometimes I would take a snack up and while I ate, a piece would fall through the vent down upon them. They would look up and tell me to get back to bed.

I'd like you to consider looking at chakra energies like that vent. The energy of chakras flows between the ground floor and the second floor in the building metaphor. Just as heat rises as air vibrates faster and faster, energy frequencies vibrate more slowly and become denser until they float down and create physical bodies. There are vents connecting each floor of our seven-floored house. Through these vents, finer energy flows down into more dense energy. The connection, the vents, are always there. But sometimes they aren't completely open. Our goal in chakra work is to open each vent completely.

The vent flow controls the amount of energy in each chakra. In addition, each chakra room has a door that connects to the next room. For example, here we are in the physical room of the root chakra, and we are experiencing some fears about our ability to find a job. First, we open the vent and receive more energy from above through meditation and chakra work. We meditate to calm our minds and control our fears. Once our fears are under control, the door to the second room, the second chakra, opens and we walk into that room. The second chakra is about relationships. We meditate again and do some techniques to open the vent and allow positive energy to flow into our relationships. And surprise, the door to the third chakra, the solar plexus, opens. That chakra is all about personal power. We quickly open that vent above, and with the increased energy we receive we may learn some tai chi to give us confidence and that feeling of power. When we realize that power is nothing without love, we center our meditations on power with positive regard and loving kindness, and the door into the heart chakra room opens. The opening of one room leads to another, constantly being fed energy from the corresponding room on the second floor above. The throat chakra room of creative energy opens with positive affirmations and powerful statements of your own creativity, your own value. The brow chakra room of soul force and intuition opens through mindfulness or insight meditation. By becoming aware of our thoughts, we have the power to see beyond them into other aspects of our consciousness. We have the power to now explore other rooms of our building and to go back into any room we wish at any time we need that specific energy. This is a simplified way of saying that when working with chakras, keep in mind the chakra circulation and balance within you as well as the energy flows coming into you.

Each floor in the metaphor of our house also has a vent to the next higher floor that chakra energy as chi, energy, soul energy, or Higher Self energy passes through. Chakras are the energy of *you* in a higher vibration. Chakras are where *you* meets you. The you that vibrates higher wants all good to manifest in your life. However, the denser physical you sometimes tries to close off the vent and prevent this higher energy from coming through. That's why it's important to keep the vents open on all levels, or at least as many as we can as often as we can. The building, rooms, and floors imagery is helpful in remembering that we have energy circulating inside us as well as higher, less dense Source energy dampening down into the mental, emotional, and physical at all times. We truly are sunbeams and waves of light and love.

One of the most valuable works we can do is to learn how to take responsibility for and allow pure chakra energy into our lives. In this chapter we explore each chakra in depth and practice techniques for releasing negativity and inviting the full flow of positive chakra energy into our lives.

Overview of the Chakras

Chakra evolution can be traced from our ancestors to present day. The first chakra to develop fully was the root chakra. This energy system lies at the base of the spine and is concerned primarily with survival on the physical plane. Early cave dwellers had to utilize this energy to simply exist in a dangerous world. Root chakra energy is about taking the responsibility to live in a physical world. It's the energy for survival, security, health, money, and even death when the time comes. The energy of this chakra flows today when we return to the land via nature, gardening, hiking, walking barefoot, and engaging in physical activities that in involve the body and mind.

As physical needs were met, social relationships began to develop. Sensuality and sexuality between two people expanded to include pleasure and gratification available from others. Societies were built on the energy of the pelvic second chakra. Today we experience this energy when in community with others. The demonstrations for change in the world are a charged by the energy of this second chakra.

Once human beings had established safety and community, the personal power of the third chakra began developing in the solar plexus area. This is a masculine power of aggressiveness, competitiveness, recognition, status, self-image, and significance. Civilizations advanced and fell according to the dominating individual or ego involved. This chakra has been dominant since the middle of the twentieth century. When this chakra is abused, a narcissistic, power-hungry person emerges. When used with other chakra energies, philanthropists are seen.

The love-ins of the 1960s, more than anything else, express the emergence of the fourth chakra, the heart. Opening of the heart chakra allows self-acceptance and generates feelings of love and caring for others as well as oneself. This feminine center balances the self-preoccupation of the lower centers and acts as a bridge to higher emotions and energies. There is always a tug between love and fear. Fear rests in the lower three chakras. Love takes us to the higher three chakras.

As we continue to move into the twenty-first century, the throat chakra has many of us literally choking! The opening of our creative abilities of self-expression is the next major lesson for many of us. This chakra of communication is seen in the growing of the internet, social media, smartphone apps, and communication with artificial intelligence, like Apple's Siri and Amazon's Alexa. Instantaneous global communication challenges us to our highest levels of creativity and integration.

The brow chakra is the witness center, the joining of left and right brain wisdom and intelligence. The energies here connect us with our higher self and encourage the development and practical use of intuition. There have been individuals throughout history who have focused on the brow and crown chakras. But mostly they have been isolated in ashrams, temples, monasteries. The next step in today's world is for this chakra to open up in the secular world.

Our spiritual center is located at the crown of the head and is our connection with cosmic consciousness. The energy here enables us to live in the moment, without desire. To be truly free of concerns, worries, doubts, and fears.

Exceptions to the rule of chakra development have occurred throughout history. Jesus, the Buddha, and other wise and holy people through the ages have demonstrated full mastery of all chakras. In fact, we all have access to all the power of our chakras at any given moment. We all have had experiences of unconditional love, of a sense of oneness with the beauty of our environment, of pure joy.

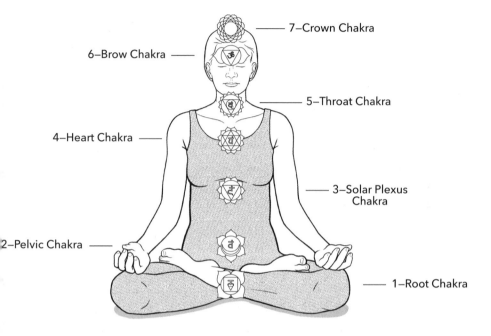

7–Crown Chakra, at top of head, reaching back to Source Energy

6–Brow Chakra, at forehead between the eyebrows, intuition and insight

5–Throat Chakra, at t hroat area, communication and creativity

4–Heart Charka, at heart area, unconditional love and healing

3–Solar Plexus Chakra, just below the rib cage, personal power

2–Pelvic Chakra, in pelvic area, relationships and sexuality

1–Root Chakra, at base of spine reaching down into the earth, material safety and well-being

Chakra Figure

Practice
Chakra Color Visualization

A simple practice to begin enlivening your chakras is color imagery. Before going to sleep each night, take a couple of minutes to complete the following visualization. Begin by imagining a soft glow of red at the base of your spine. Notice the quality of the color and make it bright and beautiful. Now allow this red color to expand and flow up your body, down your arms and legs, and up into your head. Continue to allow red to expand through and out your body, surrounding you in a gentle red glow.

Repeat this process using the following colors and areas: orange in the pelvis, yellow in the solar plexus, green in the heart, blue in the throat, indigo at the brow, violet at the top of your head, and white surrounding your whole being. As you work with these colors, allow your breath to move the energy through and around you. Slow your breathing and let the colors flow and merge. Perform this practice nightly and notice differences in feelings, sensations, and attitudes. Color imagery is one of the first steps you can take to begin to explore and balance the chakra energies within you.

Our purpose now is to learn how to fully utilize chakra energy for the highest good of our family, our community, the earth, and ourselves. This requires learning how to let go of negative emotions and conditions that disturb the flow of our energies and learning how to refine and develop these energies for consistent positive manifestation in our world.

The Root Chakra and Our Basic Needs

Root Chakra, Muladhara, Support	
Location: Base of spine	**To Balance**
Keywords: Life, strength, power	**Color:** Wear red, sit under a red light, look into a red painting, eat red-skinned fruits and vegetables
Action: Will to live and physical vitality; kinesthetic, proprioceptive, and tactile senses	
Goal: Mastery of the body so it may be used as a tool for Spirit	**Sound:** Solfeggio frequency 369 Hz for liberating guilt and fear
Glands and Organs: Spinal column, adrenals, kidneys, rectum, legs, bones, feet	**Gemstones:** Garnet, ruby, coral, jasper, tiger's eye, smoky quartz, obsidian, pyrite, agate
Color: Red	**Imagery:** Imagine yourself traveling deep into the earth, releasing all fears into the dark, moist earth.
Sound: LAM	
Note: C	**Ceremony and Ritual:** Write down all your fears, then burn the paper, saving the ashes. Now write down your desires and bury them, spreading the ashes to fertilize your desires.
Element: Earth	
Planet: Sun and moon	
Unbalanced: Role confusion, fear, martyrdom, anger, self-pressuring, anemia, iron deficiency, low blood pressure, decreased muscle tone, fatigue, adrenal insufficiency	
Balanced: Affection, generosity, sensitivity to others, physical strength, higher action to break mental conditioning, rapid change toward physical health	

Qualities

The root chakra is located between the legs, its tip seated in the sacral-coccyx joint at the bottom of the tailbone. Imagine a ball of sparkling red energy sitting between the bottom of your spine and your genitals. Called *muladhara*, "support," this chakra's energy represents life, strength, power, and vitality. The energy to meet our basic needs resides here. This area is the key to grounding our dreams in the material world and in transforming etheric energy into observable reality. This is the universal life force, the kundalini serpent of wisdom and life, lying coiled, ready to rise.

Our energy goal here is to "become master of the body so it can be used as a tool for Spirit."[30] When we are struggling ourselves, it is hard to do good in the world. When we are afraid that the bank will take away our house or that our bodies may have cancer, it is difficult to live our lives in peace. And peace in the world begins with peace within us.

The root chakra is associated with the color red, the note C, the sound LAM, the element earth, the sun, and the moon. Its energy is reflected in the spinal column, adrenal glands, kidneys, rectum, legs, bones, feet, and immune system. For example, when a client has a stress issue, I look for hyperactive adrenal glands and work directly with the energy of the root chakra for grounding. The root chakra is strengthened by family bonds that provide a sense of safety and security. The family need not be connected by blood. More and more people are looking for a group who will help them feel safe and cared for in this world. Fear is the major block to the energy (chi) of the root chakra. Fear of material loss, injury, disease, death, limitation, loneliness. The desire for protection is the overall emotion of the root chakra. Psychological imbalance in the root chakra may manifest as role confusion, fear, martyrdom, anger, self-pressuring, greed, cruelty, and over-impulsiveness. Physical imbalance may manifest as anemia, iron deficiency, low blood pressure, decreased muscle tone, fatigue, and adrenal insufficiency.

Balanced, clear, and bright, this basic energy provides affection, generosity, sensitivity to others, ambition to better oneself, and strong physical propensities. Balancing the root chakra results in the ability to take higher action to break mental conditioning and rapid change toward physical well-being.

....

30. Alex S. Jones, *Seven Mansions of Color* (Millbrook, Ontario: Cygnet Publications, 2015), 19.

Because this chakra contains old belief patterns that may still have authority in our lives, balancing it may require careful introspection. Beliefs about our body, our health, and our money are deeply ingrained in us. When we work with the root chakra, we work to change our beliefs about the very basic issues of our lives. We pledge to release beliefs that hinder us, and we open to beliefs that fulfill our lives.

Practice
Activities and Rituals to Balance the Root Chakra

Below are some guidelines to assist you in balancing this vital energy that supplies your basic needs.

The Color Red: Use the color red in your environment to stimulate will and life force, overcome depression, and bring about positive change. Wear red, sit under a red light, look into a red painting, and eat red-skinned fruits and vegetables like cherries, strawberries, radishes, beets, and tomatoes. Use your creativity to bring more red into your life!

Music: Singing or listening to music in the key of C works well here.

Chanting: Chant the sacred sound LAM to bring energy into the root chakra and open up the flow. Say or sing LAM slowly on as long an outbreath as is comfortable for you. Feel the grounding energy and repeat as necessary.

Gemstones: Play with gemstones. The following is a partial listing of gemstones associated with the first chakra: garnet, ruby, coral, jasper, red tiger's eye, smoky quartz, obsidian, pyrite, and red agate. Place one of these stones in your pocket and each time you touch it, affirm your physical vitality and material well-being. Sleep with a stone in your hand all night to allow your subconscious to affirm your willingness to accept improvement in all conditions associated with this chakra.

Visualization: Imagine traveling deep into the earth and planting there all your desires for material wellness. Release all fears and worries and use them as fertilizer for these new conditions that will manifest into your life. Perhaps you may wish to actually do just that! Write down all the beliefs you wish to release, then tear up the paper or burn it, saving the scraps or ashes. Now write down all the desires you wish to manifest. Bury these desires in the ground, intact, and spread your fertilizer around them. For out of the ashes rises the phoenix.

It is wise to attend to the energy of the root chakra when you are feeling spacey and out of sorts. When the plans you have made do not come to fruition, when you are feeling physically tired or ill, when you are constantly worried or fearful, then look to this energy at the base of your spine.

The root chakra is particularly difficult for many of us. We have great ideas in our heads but have a hard time grounding them in reality! We may be experiencing chronic health difficulties, chronic financial worries, or other conditions that underlie our basic fears. Becoming aware of the energy of the root chakra and using the activities listed in this chapter can help open up this vital earth energy. Pay particular attention to the mental attitudes and emotional feelings you may be holding on to in this area. Opening this chakra may be as simple as watching a movie that comforts you or spending a day in nature, sitting under a tree. You know when you are balanced in the root chakra when you truly feel safe and secure. If you do not feel that way now, find small ways to bring these feelings into your life and then let them grow bigger and stronger. In Spirit, you are safe and secure, always. Now allow that feeling of Spirit to enter your daily affairs. Patience and practice will give you results!

The Pelvic Chakra and Our Relationships

Pelvic Chakra, Svadhisthana, Vital Force	
Location: Just above the pubic bone on the front and back of the body; its tip goes into the center of the sacrum	**To Balance**
Keywords: Sexual energy, creative energy	**Color:** Wear orange, decorate study rooms, style meeting places with orange color
Action: Center of emotions related to relationships, sensuality, and sexuality	**Sound:** Solfeggio frequency of 417 Hz resonates with the 8 Hz of the Schumann frequency, deeply calming and soothing earth frequency healing
Goal: Performance of one's duties without attachment to fruits of action	**Gemstones:** Carnelian, agate
Glands and Organs: Sexual organs, immune system	**Imagery:** Imagine yourself floating down a gentle river: release all attachments, float, observe, and let go.
Color: Orange	**Ceremony and Ritual:** Write down your attachments on a piece of biodegradable paper, shape them into a boat, and place the boat in a moving stream of water. Watch and let go!
Sound: VAM	
Note: D	
Element: Water	
Planets: Moon, Venus	
Unbalanced: Greed, abandonment, defensiveness, self-consciousness, weakened immune system, muscle spasms	
Balanced: Sexual energy, creative energy	

Qualities

The pelvic chakra, sometimes referred to as the sacral chakra, is located just above the pubic bone on the front and back of the body. Its tip goes into the center of the sacrum. Imagine an orange ball of sparkling energy sitting here. In Chinese medicine it is called the lower dantian, *dan t'ian*, or *dan tien* and translated as "sea of qi" or "the place of Source Energy" that feeds the entire body. Known as *svadisthana*, "vital force" in Hindu, the pelvic chakra represents optimism, self-confidence, enthusiasm, and courage. The social ray of service to humankind resides here. This area is the key to centering our emotions of sensuality and sexuality. This is the chakra of duality, yin and yang, and understanding the significance of opposites, especially ourselves in relation to society.

The goal of this second chakra is the "performance of one's duties for God without a self-motivation or attachment to the fruits of action."[31] We simply do what we do without waiting for praise or reward. The pelvic chakra is associated with the color orange, the note D, the sound VAM, the element water, the moon, and the planet Venus. Its energy is reflected in the sexual organs, large intestine, lower vertebrae, pelvis, hip area, appendix, and bladder. Clients who have low back pain often are having problems in their relationships. Both of these physical and emotional areas may stem from a disturbance of energy in the pelvic chakra. I check there first.

Known as the chakra of relationships, the pelvic chakra provides endurance to sustain relationships, whether at work for financial reasons, at home for family, or in community. This is the momma lion defending her pride. Blocks in the second chakra may result in attachment to our doings like substance abuse, compulsiveness, food cravings, necessity to be liked or loved at all costs, or sexual desires beyond the norm.

Psychological imbalance in the pelvic chakra may manifest as greed, fears of abandonment, defensiveness, self-consciousness, and narcissistic personality disorders. Physical imbalance may manifest as sexual disorders, immune system dysfunction, muscle spasms, and weakness.

Balanced, clear, and bright, this orange energy provides optimism, hospitality, and humanitarianism. Balancing the second chakra results in the ability to overcome suspicion, insecurity, and lack of trust and the power to follow

....

31. Jones, *Seven Mansions of Color*, 20.

good rules and overcome bad habits. The pelvic chakra contains belief patterns associated with our sense of self, our sexuality, and our relationships to society. It is the chakra of attachments. Having developed to some extent a comfortable relationship with our own bodies, we now reach out to explore others. We become attached to our mate, our house, and our position in society. Any change disrupts our sense of self, and we spend a lot of time avoiding all change. This avoidance dampens our creativity and our ability to go beyond our present conditions.

The work of the pelvic chakra is about taking risks, taking charge of our lives. It is about choosing our companions wisely and gently allowing the negative to leave our lives. Remember that the element water is associated with this chakra. Discover in the pelvic chakra how to let go and flow. We detach from our addictions to food, drink, and drugs and from our addictions to people, places, and things.

An affirmation I have found helpful and repeat often is "I relax, I release, I let go, and I flow in the spirit of love."

Practice
Activities and Rituals to
Balance the Pelvic Chakra

The following are some guidelines to assist you in balancing this orange energy, which supplies your relationship needs.

The Color Orange: Use the color orange in your environment to stimulate social enterprise and creativity. Orange is a social color and good in community centers, meeting places, areas of creative study, and hospital rooms. An orange wardrobe will fill you with feelings of courage and optimism. Eat orange-skinned fruits and vegetables like oranges, tangerines, and carrots. Use your creativity to bring more orange into your life!

Music: Singing or listening to music in the key of D works well here.

Chanting: Say or sing VAM slowly on as long an outbreath as is comfortable for you. Feel the flowing energy and repeat as necessary.

Gemstones: Play with gemstones. Carnelian is the most common gemstone associated with the second chakra. Place a carnelian stone in your pocket and each time you touch it, affirm your physical vitality and material well-being. Sleep with a stone in your hand all night to allow your subconscious to affirm your willingness to accept improvement in all conditions associated with relationships and creativity.

Visualization: Imagine floating down a gentle river. Release all attachments by making them part of the passing landscape. You observe and you let go. Call to mind all things you think you must have to be happy and let each go. If you have a moving body of water near you—a creek, stream, or river, write down your attachments on a piece of environmentally friendly paper. Shape the paper into a boat and watch your attachments float away from your life.

Energy Work: Open up the lower dantian source of chi located between the belly button and lower lumbar vertebrae, specifically L5. In chi gong we release stagnant energy and absorb clean universal chi energy through gentle movements and intentions. This release and absorb is like performing an energy oil change. One of our main problems in life is absorbing everyone else's energy and not releasing what is not for our highest good. I first learned about absorb-release from Master Luke Chan, and the following is my adaptation of his program.[32]

Sit and place your hands on your belly, with your middle fingers on your navel. Now gently open your arms, with hands relaxed to a comfortable width, as if you were holding a beach

32. Luke Chan, "6 Dimensional Self-Healing Gongs," Chi-Lel Qigong, accessed January 12, 2022, https://www.lukechanchilel.com/course/6-dimensional-self-healing-gongs/.

ball in front of you. While opening, imagine that you are releasing any stale energy, any energy that is no longer necessary to your well-being. The practice routine goes like this:

Exhale while opening your hands and arms out in front of you as if holding the beach ball. Imagine releasing all the old, stale energy that has been cluttering up your mind and body.

After slowly releasing for several seconds, inhale and reverse the motion, as if you were gently collapsing the beach ball, and draw fresh universal energy back into you. Visualize absorbing fresh, clean energy back into your whole body on the inbreath.

Use your hands and mind in this way to release and renew. You may find your whole body getting into the motion, flexing the trunk and shoulders forward as you move your arms out and straightening your posture upward as you absorb in. You may spend several minutes or several hours doing this technique. You may use this method to open and cleanse any chakra area by moving your hands to that area and repeating the process.

Difficulties with relationships, difficulties with sensuality and sexuality, and resentment and blame of others indicate blocks in this chakra. This chakra is often closed by early negative experiences with groups. Do you remember trying to be with the in-crowd in high school or experiencing difficulty on your first job, again the issue of fitting in?

To open this chakra often requires acts of forgiveness. Use gentle meditations to release past hurts and resentments. Sometimes it requires a change of attitude about people and society. I like the model used by the Nature Conservancy. Instead of condemning society for the destruction of natural habitats, or organizing protests, the Nature Conservancy simply goes about quietly buying land. When they see land that is going to be used for a potentially harmful activity, they buy it. They do not use hate or anger. They quietly make a difference because they know that if they own the land, then they can use it to benefit nature and the earth.

You, too, can quietly make a difference in your relationships. Change your attitude and accomplish your goals in a new way. This is the message of the second chakra.

The Solar Plexus Chakra and Personal Power

Solar Plexus Chakra, Manipura, Jewel	
Location: At the bottom of the rib cage, between thoracic vertebra T12 and lumbar vertebra L1	**To Balance**
	Color: Wear yellow, sit under the sun, bring yellow flowers into your room
Keywords: Mental power, happiness, joy	*Sound:* 528 Hz, heal and repair the body by reducing stress in the endocrine and autonomic nervous systems. Called the miracle frequency.
Action: Related to who we are and our own personal power	
Goal: Control over body and mind	
Glands and Organs: Stomach, liver, gall bladder, pancreas, spleen, nervous system	*Gemstones:* Yellow citrine, amber, light smoky quartz, yellow jade
Color: Yellow	*Imagery:* Imagine lying on a beach in the sun. The warm rays of the sun shine down upon you, relaxing and healing!
Sound: RAM	
Note: E	
Element: Fire	*Ceremony and Ritual:* Write out your personal mission statement on yellow paper and post it on yellow notes everywhere. Remind yourself why you are here!
Planet: Mercury	
Unbalanced: Worry, anger, anxiety, decreased intelligence, digestive disorders, sinus and allergy disorders, skin disorders, blood sugar disorders	
Balanced: Increased force of will, warmth, male energy to manifest	

Qualities

The tip of the solar plexus chakra is seated just below the ribcage in the center of the body. Follow your breastbone down to its base—that's where the diaphragm attaches. The chakra is there between the front and back of the body, between thoracic vertebra T12 and lumbar vertebra L1. Imagine a sparkling ball of yellow energy sitting here. Called *manipura*, "jewel," it represents mental or intellectual power, happiness, and joy. Sometimes referred to as the yellow Christ ray of wisdom, this area is the key to expressing our personal power. Our actions become motivated by the inspiration of vision and reason and are performed with the qualities of patience and self-control.

The goal of the third chakra is control and discipline over the body and mind to combine our own personal power with the "power of Spirit within us."[33] The solar plexus chakra is associated with the color yellow, the note E, the sound RAM, the element fire, and the planet Mercury. Its energy is reflected in the stomach, liver, gallbladder, pancreas, spleen, and the nervous system. The solar plexus chakra is the energy of self-esteem, self-respect, and self-discipline. This action chakra gives us the ability handle crisis and the courage to take risks. Disruption of the energy here erupts in anger, aggressiveness, hostility, and frustration on the one hand and worthlessness, helplessness, emptiness, and feelings of being mistreated or not getting the credit one deserves on the other hand.

Psychological imbalance in the solar plexus chakra may manifest as worry, anxiety, and decreased mental sharpness or narcissistic aggressive behaviors on the other hand. Physical imbalance may manifest as digestive disorders, sinus and allergy problems, skin disorders, and blood sugar disorders.

Balanced, the solar plexus chakra provides an increased force of will, warmth, and the male energy to manifest. Balancing the third chakra results in high creativity, great precision and analytical abilities, flexibility and adaptability to change, efficiency in planning and organizing work, and effectiveness in problem-solving. The solar plexus chakra contains belief patterns we hold about ourselves. It is the chakra of the personality or ego. In this chakra we typically experience the world as either "good for me" or "bad for me." Events and people who are good for me bring joy; those who are bad for me bring anger. The element fire rules this chakra, and the fire of the ego is often felt here.

....

33. Jones, *Seven Mansions of Color*, 22.

Another issue in this chakra is the issue of power. Many people shy away from the notion of power. Power often represents embedded established rules for the few, not the many, and frequently produces injustice. It is more than time now to claim our true power—the power to heal and change the world. This power is not from the ego but from higher guidance and wisdom. With true personal power we become leaders and world servers and truly fulfill our missions here.

Practice
Activities and Rituals to
Balance the Solar Plexus Chakra

The following are some guidelines to assist you in developing an authentic personal power.

Mission Statement: Write your personal mission statement using yellow legal paper, of course! This approach is adapted from a technique in Laurie Beth Jones's book *The Path*.[34] First determine two to four action verbs that describe what you do. Use power words such as *empower, serve, extend*, and *promote*. I selected a few words, then looked up each in the thesaurus, and then looked up what I found. It took several sessions until I found the words that invoked a passion in me when reading them. Next, list what these words apply to healing, teaching, love, and peace. And finally, state who you are going to be with when you are performing your mission, such as friends, the government, a business, groups, and so on. Your mission statement must be bold enough to inspire you and broad enough to apply to all aspects of your life.

Using this procedure, I developed the following mission statement for myself: "My mission is to explore, facilitate, and advance well-being in myself, individuals, groups, and organizations." This

---

34. Laurie Beth Jones, *The Path: Creating Your Mission Statement for Work and for Life* (New York: Hachette Books, 1998).

statement applies to my own inner explorations and to my public roles as an energy worker, a storekeeper, a meditation instructor, and a professional educational consultant. I use it as my daily focus.

The Color Yellow: Use the color yellow in your environment to stimulate your joy of living. Yellow is the color of intellect and is good in libraries and study rooms. A yellow wardrobe will fill you with feelings of joy and security. Eat yellow-skinned fruits and vegetables like corn, squash, lemons, bananas, pineapples, grapefruit, and melons.

Music: Singing or listening to music in the key of E works well here.

Chanting: Chant the sacred word RAM out loud to bring power to your center. Say or sing RAM slowly on as long an out-breath as is comfortable for you. Feel the empowering energy and repeat as necessary.

Gemstones: Play with gemstones, especially yellow citrine, amber, gold tiger's eye, light smoky quartz, and yellow jade. Place one of these stones in your pocket and each time you touch it, affirm your power to fulfill your mission and live your dreams. Sleep with a stone in your hand all night to allow your subconscious to affirm your willingness to accept genuine personal power in your life.

Power Place: Think back to a time you felt powerful in your life, powerful in a good way. Maybe you helped a project get off the ground. Maybe you taught a group a new technique that made their jobs or their lives easier. Maybe it was a time when you were athletic or were peaceful in the midst of a storm. One of my powerful moments I can remember was water skiing behind a boat on the Ohio River. The river was calm and reflected the setting sun like glass. I was on my single water ski, cutting back and forth across the boat's wake. I owned the water, the river, the ski. I was in my element. I was powerful. Find your power place and bring that emotion, that feeling, back into your life today just by thinking about it. Shifting your energy from weakness into strength is a very powerful thing to do. In fact, it may be the most powerful thing you can do to better your life!

Our ability to make our way in this world, to be empowered to action, to reach our goals, lies in the solar plexus chakra. Misuse of this energy results in ego domination and domination over others. You know when the power is being misused when actions are motivated by anger, jealousy, and fear. When you feel better than everyone else or look down on other people. Misaligned solar plexus energy creates the roles of victim and persecutor. Many people jump between these roles and wonder why they always feel bad, between the roles of total authority and narcissism to the "poor me" victim when someone or something goes against their wishes. This is a hard way to live. Correct use of solar plexus energy results in having the ability to effect change for the better in our lives and the lives around us. The feeling of power comes from deep within—a power to do right. We are all powerful. Most of us who do not feel powerful run the risk of being taken advantage of by those who have developed their power without love and compassion. Opening and clearing the energy of the solar plexus enables us to use our power for the highest good of all concerned.

The Heart Chakra and Love and Healing

Heart Charka, Anahata, Unbeaten	
Location: Heart and chest area	**To Balance**
Keywords: Love, balance, peacemaking, hope, growth, healing	**Color:** Wear green, bring green plants into your home or business, eat green vegetables and fruits
Action: Front aspect is love; rear aspect is will	**Sound:** 639 Hz, bringing love and healing into our lives
Goal: To use the force of love for personal and societal change	**Gemstones:** Emerald, peridot, tourmaline, jade, malachite, green calcite, aventurine, bloodstone, fluorite, unakite, rose quartz, rhodochrosite, coral, garnet
Glands and Organs: Heart, circulatory system, thymus, vagus nerve, upper back	
Color: Green	**Imagery:** Imagine a tiny spark of light deep in your heart area. Allow this light to grow, warming, healing. See it expand to warm and heal all around you.
Sound: YAM	
Note: F	
Element: Air	
Planet: Jupiter	**Ceremony and Ritual:** Write our affirmations of love, such as "I love and accept myself" or "May all beings be filled with loving kindness." Repeat loving affirmations often.
Unbalanced: Crisis, mood swings, panic, speeding heart rate, palpitation, arrythmias, panic attacks	
Balanced: Generosity, nurturing, calming, relaxing and expanding, strengthening heart, prosperity	

Qualities

The heart chakra surrounds the area of the physical heart. Called *anahata*, "unbeaten," this chakra represents the emotional power of love. Imagine a ball of radiant green energy sitting in the area of your heart. The middle dantian energy center sits behind the heart level, at the seventh thoracic vertebra. In the Chinese energy system, the middle dantian controls the energy of the heart and lungs. This area is the key to balance, harmony, peacemaking, hope, growth, healing, and love. Our actions become motivated by the quality of unconditional love, acceptance of self and others, and right use of compassion.

The goal of the fourth chakra is to allow love and compassion to guide all our actions in this world, bringing about a state of Divine Love being "manifested in everyone."[35] The heart chakra is associated with the color green, the note F, the sound YAM, the element air, and the planet Jupiter. Its energy is reflected in the heart, circulatory system, ribs, breasts, thymus gland, lungs, vagus nerve, shoulders, arms, and upper back. The heart chakra is our source for loving kindness, forgiveness, compassion, hope, trust, and the ability to heal ourselves and others. Frequencies that muddy the energy of the heart include jealousy, hatred, shame, loneliness, sadness, grief, isolation, and shame.

Psychological imbalance in the heart chakra may manifest as crisis, mood swings, intense grief, and general panic. Physical imbalance may manifest as speeding heart rate, palpitation, arrythmias, difficulty breathing, lung problems, and panic attacks.

Balanced, the heart chakra provides generosity, nurturing, calming, relaxing, expanding, and strengthening of the heart and lungs. Balancing the fourth chakra results in feelings of brotherhood and sisterhood, prosperity, helpfulness, and unconditional love. These qualities help us uplift others so they may also love and respect themselves.

The heart chakra contains belief patterns we hold about life itself. It is the chakra that teaches the lesson of forgiveness. Through the years we have learned to place emphasis on conditions for loving and being loved. Many of us grew up feeling not good enough and believing that if only we could do or be something else, we would be loved. With each action we asked, "If I do this for you, will you love me?" And with each disappointment we became bitter and resentful.

....

35. Jones, *Seven Mansions of Color*, 22.

Opening the heart chakra involves learning to love without dependency on external cause. Learning to love simply because we are love. Learning to forgive because we know that we are Spirit and cannot be harmed. Unconditional love means to accept others and ourselves without judgment or attachment. Loving simply because that is what we naturally do. This is no easy task, and we all have daily opportunities to practice giving love. When a person is angry or hurting, they are asking for love. And when we can give love regardless of their behavior, then we have practiced one of our major life lessons.

Practice
Activities and Rituals to
Balance the Heart Chakra

The following are some guidelines to assist you in developing an unconditional love.

Affirmations: Write out affirmations of love and acceptance, first of yourself, then of others. If you can love and accept yourself and stop with all the "should have, would have," there is nothing to forgive, and there is nothing to do but share your love with others. I find this so much harder to do than to say. It feels like hundreds of times a day I am judging myself for what I am doing and what I am not doing. Our unloving egos set us up so that we can't win either way. The only exit out of judgment is affirming love. I love myself. I accept myself. I am doing the best I can at this moment in my life and I am loving and well. And only when I'm in a loving state can I truly love another. It's worth the work!

Music: Singing or listening to music in the key of F goes well here.

Chanting: Say or sing YAM slowly on as long an outbreath as is comfortable for you. Feel the loving energy and repeat as necessary.

The Color Green: Use the color green in your environment to stimulate healing, well-being, and prosperity. Green promotes a sense of rest and relaxation and is good in bedrooms, hospital rooms, and meeting rooms where love is needed. A green wardrobe brings balance and harmony and fills you with feelings of serene, calming peace. Eat green fruits and vegetables, including lettuce, green beans, broccoli, asparagus, green peas, spinach, limes, green apples, honeydew melons, and so on.

Pink is also a good color for the heart. If you blend the red of the root chakra with the white of the crown chakra, the result is perfect pink, sitting at the heart chakra bridge between the lower three chakras and the upper three chakra energies.

Gemstones: Play with gemstones, especially emerald, peridot, tourmaline, jade, malachite, green calcite, aventurine, bloodstone, fluorite, and unakite. Place these stones in your pocket and each time you touch them, affirm your power to love unconditionally. Sleep with a stone in your hand all night to allow your subconscious to affirm your willingness to accept genuine love in your life.

Awakening the Heart and Lungs: Open up the middle dantian by exercising your shoulder blades, the scapulae. Luke Chan of Chi-Lel Qigong describes three motions, or six directions, that occur to open the energy that feeds the heart and lungs.[36] Practice the following without strain. You can start with slowly moving each direction nine times, gradually adding more repetitions. Sit with your hands over your navel.

Direction 1: Move your shoulder blades forward and backward. Imagine the wheels of a bicycle turning.

Direction 2: Move your shoulder blades up and down. Imagine shrugging and then relaxing your shoulders.

Direction 3: Move your shoulder blades left and right. Imagine the steering wheel of a car turning gently left and right.

....

36. Luke Chan, "Introduction: Lungs Chi Massage," Chi-Lel Qigong, May 2016, https://www.lukechanchilel.com/lesson/introduction-lungs-chi-massage-2/.

Meditate: Meditate using this ancient Tibetan Buddhist loving kindness blessing or a loving blessing you create on your own. Notice that you give the blessing to yourself first. Once you feel well, peaceful, and happy, your vibrations will naturally give those feelings to another person. Once you both feel that way, you both may give the blessings outward to all beings. This is how we bless and change the world. Say it, sing it, feel it, believe it.

May I be filled with loving kindness
May I be well
May I be peaceful and at ease
May I be happy

May you be filled with loving kindness
May you be well
May you be peaceful and at ease
May you be happy

May all beings be filled with loving kindness
May all beings be well
May all beings be peaceful and at ease
May all beings be happy

Opening the heart to love may take a lifetime—or several. It is often easier for us to love our children or our pets than it is to love ourselves. Yet the paradox is that we can only give others the love we feel inside.

Some of us have learned to love ourselves too much, expecting others to do what we want when we want it. Some of us have grown up with feelings of not being good enough or worthy of love. Some have confused *eros*, erotic love, and *philia*, brotherly love, with *agape*, divine love of the highest. Both eros and philia love are generated from the heart and the lower three chakras. Agape love is love from the higher three chakras. It is love from our Source, which is God, the Source, the creator of all things. When we can tap into Source love, through meditation or deep caring and compassion, we naturally share that love with all beings. We have then awakened the heart chakra to a wonderful new universe of love.

The Throat Chakra and Expression

Throat Chakra, Visshuddha, Pure	
Location: In front and back of the throat, tip is seated in cervical vertebra C3	**To Balance**
Keywords: Inspiration, creativity, spiritual understanding	**Color:** Wear blue and use blue in your environment. Blue relaxes the mind!
Action: Giving and receiving and speaking our truth	**Sound:** 741 Hz, cleansing the body-mind and allowing us to speak our truth
Goal: To establish the kingdom of peace and share it with others	**Gemstones:** Turquoise, celestite, aquamarine, blue topaz, amazonite, blue agate, dumortierite
Glands and Organs: Thyroid, bronchi, lungs, esophagus	**Imagery:** Sit quietly and observe your breath coming and going from your nose and mouth. Just be with the breath, letting all else go, mindful of the breath.
Color: Blue	
Sound: HAM	
Note: G	**Ceremony and Ritual:** Sleep with a blue stone in your hand at night. This allows your subconscious to activate your power of expression.
Element: Ether	
Planet: Saturn	
Unbalanced: Fear of success, power, frustration, respiratory/bronchial problems	
Balanced: Joy, relaxation, increased visualization, communication, open channel between heart and brow	

Qualities

The throat chakra is in the front and back of the throat area, its tip seated in the third cervical vertebrae on the neck just below the base of the skull. Called *visshuddha*, "pure," this chakra represents the emotional power of expression. Imagine a ball of sparkling light blue energy enlivening your throat. This area is the key to giving and receiving and to speaking our truth. Our actions become motivated by the qualities of inspiration, creativity, spiritual understanding, faith, and devotion.

The goal of the fifth chakra is not only to improve communications with others in the physical world but also to communicate more directly with our souls, Higher Selves, inner wisdom, Holy Spirit, the Divine Feminine, the Divine Masculine, or whatever name you are comfortable with.[37] To go inside seeking and finding a new state of tranquility.

The throat chakra is associated with the color blue, the note G, the sound HAM, the element ether, and the planet Saturn. Its energy is reflected in the thyroid, bronchi, lungs, esophagus, neck vertebrae, mouth, jaw, and teeth. Our self-knowledge and decision-making strengths live here. We've all made decisions following our outer, ego selves that have not turned out well. The throat chakra energy allows us to go inside and consult, if you will, with that higher, wiser Self who advises us when we take time to listen. Creativity, that feeling when you are in the flow while doing a project and find the project turns out so much better than expected. You look at it and say, "Wow, I really did that? It's wonderful or beautiful or fantastic." Our inner beings are creative and not confined to the rules we have learned. Accessing the throat chakra energy allows all that creativity to flow through us and out into the world.

Psychological imbalance in the throat chakra may manifest as fear of success, fear of power, and frustration. Physical imbalance may manifest as respiratory or bronchial problems; problems with the jaw, teeth, or gums; and thyroid imbalances.

Balanced, the throat chakra provides the qualities of joy, relaxation, increased visualization, and communication. The channel between the heart and brow becomes open and flowing. Balancing the fifth chakra relieves overreactions and aggressive impulses, impulse activity, and jumping from one situation to another.

....

37. Jones, *Seven Mansions of Color*, 25.

We are able to communicate more directly with our Inner Self and allow that loving, wise, and creative Inner Self to communicate in our world.

The throat chakra contains encapsulated energy in the form of words and thoughts. Our ability to truly express ourselves becomes blocked by all the old words we cling to. As our vibrations rise in frequency, the throat chakra often forms a bottleneck of energy. Many of us who have successfully dealt with the first four chakras, more or less, become caught in our attempts to open this area. We feel the energy constriction by the chronic tension in our necks, the tightness in our shoulders and jaws. We experience all these thoughts constantly running through our meditations and we are amazed sometimes at what comes out of our mouths!

Clear expression requires inner silence; the ability to control the body, moods, and habits at will; and the ability to speak clearly with a deep, spiritual understanding. What we express outwardly returns to us, increased, and the major lesson of the throat chakra is to express that which we want to receive. It seems sometimes that despite our best efforts, we continue to react to new situations in old ways, to express our past beliefs instead of our new understandings. The throat chakra is the vehicle for expression for all other chakras and is therefore connected to every detail of our lives. Old issues emerge here for us to look at and resolve. It challenges us to learn the nature of the power of choice.

Practice
Activities and Rituals to
Balance the Throat Chakra

The following are some guidelines to assist you in opening the expression of the throat.

Mindfulness: Practice mindfulness meditation. Give yourself twenty minutes each day to sit quietly, feel your breath coming and going through your nostrils, and simply observe your thoughts. Become an impartial witness to your own mental activity. Learn to observe the encapsulated energy of thought and to free it by letting it go. Watch the bubbles of your thoughts rise to the surface and dissipate. By doing this daily, you will begin to experience the power of inner silence. From this inner silence you allow your Inner Self to advise you and are able to express right action in each present moment.

Music: Singing or listening to music in the key of G works well here.

Chanting: Say or sing HAM slowly on as long an outbreath as is comfortable for you. Feel the grounding energy and repeat as necessary.

The Color Blue: Use the color blue in your environment to stimulate spiritual freedom and creativity. Blue relaxes the mind, is cooling, and can make a room seem larger. A blue wardrobe can bring a person in touch with his or her Inner Self and enables a calm and tranquil expression of ideas and information. Eat potatoes, fish, veal, and blue-skinned fruits and berries.

Gemstones: Play with gemstones, especially turquoise, celestite, aquamarine, blue topaz, amazonite, blue agate, and dumortierite. Place these stones in your pocket and each time you touch them, affirm your choice to receive inner guidance and outward expression. Sleep with a stone in your hand all night to allow your subconscious to affirm your willingness to accept activation of your power of expression.

Sing: Sing! Fill your smartphone with songs you love to sing and sing them. Sing in the car, in the shower, outside, inside, in the bathroom. The song doesn't matter as long as you are enjoying yourself singing.

Many moons ago I attended a summer camp called Camp Lenmary. I was there each summer from the fifth grade through high school, and between high school and the start of college I was a camp counselor. We sang at camp. We sang before each meal. We sang while waiting for our mail. We sang around the campfire. During our forty-year marriage, my husband learned the words to most of my camp songs because anything could start me off singing them. When I sing Camp Lenmary songs, I feel young. I feel happy. I feel empowered. I feel that I can do anything. That is what the camp did for me all those summers. Find your happy songs and sing!

Working with the throat area allows us to become free of the past. How many times have you remembered words you said or words said by others that were not of benefit to the present moment? It seems as if we are constantly talking to ourselves—and many of the words are ones of judgment, resentment, guilt, and so forth. I can recall several days when I was mentally rehearsing a conversation I had with an extremely judgmental person. I thought about what I would say to them next, what I should have said then, and what I thought about them in general. In the meantime, the energy in my throat area became dense and clogged with all those words and emotions. Through mindfulness meditation, it finally dawned on me that not only did I not want to continue this train of thinking, but also I really did not want to encounter this person in the future. It would be of no benefit to engage in another argument—to them or to me. As I began to release the need to correct them, I also released the need to relive the conversation. Now, I can barely remember what was said. This is an important lesson for one who used to love a good argument and who loved to win a point. It is truly healthier to release and forgive, and I frequently tell myself to move on and let it go.

The Brow Chakra and Inner Wisdom

Brow Chakra, Ajna, Command	
Location: On forehead and back of head, tip is seated in center of head	**To Balance**
Keywords: Wisdom, intuition, concentration, subtle energy	*Color:* Use the color indigo in your environment to call to your wisdom and intuition.
Action: Intuition, forehead = conceptual understanding; back of head = carrying out our ideas	*Sound:* 852 Hz, connecting us to our Inner Selves, intuition, and divine purpose
Goal: To balance our thoughts and feelings with higher insight and intuition	*Gemstones:* Sapphire, sodalite, lapis lazuli
Glands and Organs: Pituitary, lower brain, left eye, ears, nose, nervous system	*Imagery:* Imagine moving down through the deep indigo waters of the Gulf Stream. Move gently down and down until you merge with deep peace.
Color: Royal blue to indigo	*Ceremony and Ritual:* Practice mantra meditation. Sing the word OM. Notice as you do that your breath becomes longer, the sound becomes freer, and you feel more relaxed.
Sound: OM	
Note: A	
Element: Energy	
Planet: Uranus	
Unbalanced: Superiority, power addiction, self-absorption, substance abuse, dependency	
Balanced: Regularity, increased intuition, wisdom, concentration, eyesight, memory, meditation, increased sensitivity to subtle energy	

Qualities

The brow chakra is located on the forehead and the back of the head, the tip seated in the center of the head. Called *ajna*, "command," this chakra represents the power of transcendence. This area is the key to balanced thinking and feeling. Our actions become more consistent, with increased wisdom, intuition, concentration, and sensitivity to subtle energy.

The goal of the sixth chakra is to become aware of ourselves as one with the higher, less dense manifestations of Spirit and direct knowing through intuition.[38] For another perspective, picture a sunbeam shining down on the floor. You are that sunbeam. When you look over shoulder, you see that you are actually a beam of energy and light going upward to the sun. As the consciousness in the sunbeam travels up the beam toward the sun, it experiences being less and less dense and more and more a part of the other sunbeams. Ultimately, all sunbeams merge into the sun. That is us, all of us: the oneness of us.

The brow chakra is associated with the color indigo, the note A, the sound OM, the element energy, and the planet Uranus. Its energy is reflected in the pituitary and pineal glands, brain and neurological system, eyes, ears, and nose. The brow chakra is the energy for our intellectual abilities, inspiration, and intuitions. This is the energy of flow, a state where we don't experience ourselves doing something, or having something done to us, but simply doing.

Psychological imbalance in the brow chakra may manifest as superiority, power addiction, and self-absorption. Physical imbalance may manifest as dependency and substance abuse.

Balanced, the brow chakra provides the qualities of spiritual perception and intuition. Our consciousness is uplifted from preoccupation with the world of sensations, and we experience an awakened realization of other planes of existence and other valid realities.

The transcendence quality of the brow chakra manifests as a true transformation in our worldly outlook. Think again about living on the ground floor of the seven-story building we talked about in the chapter on meditation. When you look out the window, you see the world from a level plane. Cars still look like cars, and people look like people. You can rearrange the interior of your apartment again and again, but you are still looking out on the same world. Now imagine

....

38. Jones, *Seven Mansions of Color*, 25.

moving up to the seventh or ninety-seventh floor of the building. You look outside and now you see everything differently. Cars no longer look like cars; they look like colorful, moving geometric shapes. People look like tiny moving elements of color. Your perspective has changed. You no longer see life in the same way.

This is true transformation. It is an effortless experience of seeing all life with a broader perspective. No longer bound by thoughts and feelings from the past, we now have the ability to cocreate our world from a higher level of consciousness. We are balanced within ourselves and within our multiple worlds of energy. From this point of true power, we are able to manifest things into the now at will. Unbound from space and time, we become masters of our own reality.

Practice
Activities and Rituals to
Balance the Brow Chakra

Below are some guidelines to assist you in opening the transcendence of the brow chakra.

Mantra: Practice mantra meditation. The most basic and simple chant is to sing the word OM. Sing OOOOOOOOOMMMMMMM over and over. Notice as you do that your breath becomes longer, the sound becomes freer, and the tone changes to match your energy. Continue this for ten minutes without interruption and you are well on your way to accessing transcendent energy. OM is the universal sound of this energy.

Music: Singing or listening to music in the key of A works well here. Listen to music in the key of A or simply hum this tone.

The Color Indigo: Use the color indigo in your environment to call to your wisdom and intuition. Meditate on the color indigo and allow its energy to move through your being. Focus on the deep, blue-violet softness and richness of this color. Imagine moving down through the waters of the Gulf Stream, which are indigo in color. Move gently down and down until you become aware of a deep inner peace, the merging of your consciousness with All That Is. Rest in this peace, without words. Allow transformation to occur of its own, naturally.

Gemstones: Play with gemstones, especially sapphire, sodalite, and lapis lazuli. Place these stones in your pocket and each time you touch them, affirm your choice to effortlessly transcend the beliefs that bind you to the past. Sleep with a stone in your hand all night to allow your subconscious to affirm your willingness to live in the present moment.

From ancient times to today the brow chakra, commonly called the third eye, and its association with the pineal gland have been considered holy. In Hindu cultures a bindi of paint or jewels is placed on the brow to connect with the deep inner wisdom and retain energy. Christians place ashes on the third eye on Ash Wednesday as a reminder to turn away from sin, repent, and turn toward God. The pineal gland sits deep in the brain behind the forehead and secretes a psychotropic hormone called melatonin.[39] Melatonin provides information about the cycles of dark and light, day and night. It is considered psychotropic because how and how much or how little melatonin is released affects behavior, mood, thoughts, or perceptions. It is not uncommon to take a melatonin supplement before bed to get to sleep and perhaps dream. As the pineal gland serves as a bridge between day and night, it may also assist the brow chakra in being a bridge between our inner and outer worlds.

The pineal has been referred to by the great philosophers as the seat of the soul. This function of the pineal gland in conjunction with the energy of the brow chakra may account for mystical experiences felt once both are open and functioning fully. Perhaps that is what is meant by "letting your light shine," "the light of God shines on me," or "I'm going to let this candle shine"?

Let your light shine in whatever way is comfortable for you. And know that that light is coming from your Higher Source, your True Self, God/Goddess, All That Is. We are here on this planet to enlighten, to heal, and to make whole.

....

39. Venkatramanujan Srinivasan, "Psychoactive Drugs, Pineal Gland and Affective Disorders," *Progress in Neuro-Psychopharmacology and Biological Psychiatry* 13, no. 5 (1989): 653–64, doi:10.1016/0278-5846(89)90052-3.

The Crown Chakra and Oneness

Crown Chakra, Sahasrara, Thousand	
Location: Top of head, tip is seated in middle of top of head	**To Balance**
Keywords: Expansiveness, gentleness, calmness, harmony	**Color:** Use the color violet in your meditation and contemplation rooms
Action: Experience of direct knowing	**Sound:** 963 Hz, for higher dimensions, ascended masters, God/Goddess/ All That Is
Goal: To experience oneness with the eternal now	
Glands and Organs: Upper brain, right eye	**Gemstones:** Amethyst, clear quartz, milk quartz
Color: Deep purple to light violet to clear	**Imagery:** Intend to experience your Self and surrender to all life during meditation. Completely let go and be.
Sound: AUM	
Note: B	**Ceremony and Ritual:** Practice silent awareness of the vastness, the space, the infinite bliss found in nature. Surrender to the moment of *now*.
Element: Cosmic energy	
Planet: Neptune	
Unbalanced: Psychic attack, negativity, paranoia, insomnia, restlessness, sensory dysfunctions	
Balanced: Increased spirituality, enlightenment, subtle body healing, increased feminine energy, calmness, gentleness, expansiveness, harmony	

Qualities

The crown chakra is located on the top of the head, with its tip seated in the middle of the top of the head. Chinese refer to its acupuncture point as *baihui* or "thousand meetings" point. Commonly called *sahasrara,* "thousand," this chakra represents the experience of direct knowing. This area is the key to spiritual enlightenment. Included in its blessings are healing of the subtle body, calmness, gentleness, expansiveness, and harmony. The goal of the seventh chakra is to fulfill our purpose by allowing "divine realization, humility, and creative imagination … as consciousness retires closer to the center of the soul in the thousand-petaled lotus in the brain."[40] Connection with this chakra is essential for understanding that we are eternal spiritual beings having a physical experience.

The crown chakra is associated with the color violet, the note B, the sound AUM, the element cosmic energy, and the planet Neptune. Its energy is reflected in major body systems including the central nervous system, the muscular system, and the skin. Resting in the energy of this chakra allows us to experience a sense of oneness that goes beyond all words to describe. When we know we are one with all, there is nothing outside ourselves to fear.

Psychological imbalance in the crown chakra may manifest as psychic attack, negativity, and paranoia. Physical imbalance may manifest as insomnia, restlessness, and sensory dysfunctions.

Balanced, the crown chakra provides the qualities of divine realization, humility, and creative imagination. Our consciousness is uplifted beyond separation to the experience of oneness with all creation and the knowing that creation is nothing but our own selves.

Experience of the crown chakra energy cannot be explained in words. It is beyond duality, and words can only point to the way. Most of us have had a brief experience of this blissful energy, whether we realized it at the time or not.

In the mid-1980s, when my husband, Charlie, and I were first becoming involved in our own spiritual development, we had just a moment of this energy. We were living in Augusta, Georgia, at the time and decided that we needed to become enlightened. We reasoned that a good place to become enlightened was in the mountains. We rented a cabin for the weekend somewhere off the Blue Ridge Parkway. We arrived at night in dense fog, found the cabin, and checked

....

40. Jones, *Seven Mansions of Color,* 28.

in, only to find that the restaurant was closed and there was no TV! When we woke up the next morning, we discovered that our window looked out over a graveyard! Nevertheless, we went out looking for our enlightenment. We hiked down a gravel road looking for a waterfall. After several hours of hiking and only finding horse droppings, we returned to the cabin and called it a day. The second morning we decided to rent the horses that had obviously found the waterfall the day before. Neither one of us was an experienced horse-rider, but Charlie was put on Spitfire and I was put on Fireball. The horses took off and we went bouncing along with them. Somewhere during that ride, we both finally relaxed into the realization that the horses were totally out of control and that at any moment we would be thrown off to our deaths! And then it happened. We had given up control and were allowed to experience Truth. For a moment, or an eternity, we could not tell which and it did not matter: we became one with All. There was no separation, no difference, between us and the horses, the grass, the trees, the horizon, the earth, the sky. We were All That Is and All That Is was us. Just as suddenly as it began, the experience ended. We were back on the horses riding toward the barn. We dismounted, got in the car, checked out of the cabin, and came home. We had experienced what we intended, though not how we intended it. That, dear reader, is oneness. It has happened to you. It will happen again for all of us.

Practice
Activities and Rituals to
Balance the Crown Chakra

The following are some guidelines to assist you in opening to the oneness of the crown chakra.

Awareness: Practice silent awareness of the vastness, the space, the infinite bliss found in nature. Practice without judgment or thought, staying in the wonder of the present moment for as long as possible.

Surrender: Intend to experience your Self and surrender to all of life. Another way of saying this is "thy will be done." Practice surrendering who you think you are to the Divine presence who knows who you are. Allow yourself to realize that the real you is always safe and healed and whole and cherished and loved and protected by the Divine. All religions teach surrendering to a higher authority to gain peace of mind. Use the word God, Allah, Goddess, Source, or Creator. The words don't matter here; it's the feeling of peace that comes only after truly surrendering. It's that energetic and emotional state we get to when we say, "I don't know how to help myself." Be you in charge, and then let go. Sometimes it takes surrendering over and over and over before the miracles granted from our Creator come into our lives, but come they will when we get our own small ego selves out of the way and let our higher, trues, wiser Selves into our lives.

Music: Singing or listening to music in the key of B works well here.

Chanting: Say or sing AUM slowly on as long an outbreath as is comfortable for you. Feel the grounding energy and repeat as necessary.

The Color Violet: Use the color violet in your meditation or contemplation rooms. Meditate on the colors violet and white and allow their energy to move through your being.

Gemstone: Play with gemstones, especially amethyst and clear quartz. Place a crystal on your nightstand to remind you of the pure light of the infinite, eternal now.

Living in a state of oneness is very rare. Experiencing moments of oneness can be cultivated through meditation, nature, and even physical activity. Though I have never participated in extreme sports such as mountain climbing, parachuting, and marathons, I am convinced that the reward for these sports is that state of perfect flow, in which the participant is truly one with the mountain, the sky, or the road.

As long as we feel enclosed within our bodies, we are separate. When our spirit expands outward to include our environment, we begin to sense feelings of belonging. And when our spirit expands even farther, we know that we are one with all, eternal and safe, healed and whole. This is the lesson of the crown chakra. It is a lesson we are all destined to learn!

Practice
Rainbow of Lights Guided Meditation

We conclude this chapter on chakras with a guided meditation. Read the following aloud into an audio recorder, then listen to it. You can also have a friend read it aloud to you, or simply read it over once, then close your eyes and remember the essence.

Begin by taking several deep and full breaths. Now relax and imagine a rainbow, all the colors vivid and bright. Look at or imagine the color red. Focus completely on the color red and allow the red to enter your body, just at the base of your spine. This red is your root or grounding color of physical vitality and basic survival on the physical plane. Release any darkness or dullness, allowing all your fears to flow out the base of your spine, down into the earth. Imagine the color red becoming more brilliant, more beautiful. Allow this wonderful red to move through your entire body, from the top of your head to the tips of your toes—cleansing, revitalizing, and healing.

Focus your attention now on the color orange. Allow this light to enter your body, in the area of the pelvis. Orange is the color of your relationships with yourself, your friends, your colleagues, your community, and society. Allow all past disagreements to flow out of your body, down into the earth. Make this orange more beautiful, vibrant. See all relationships healing, becoming whole. Allow this feeling of peace and cooperation to flow through you and out into the world as the color orange fills your body from head to toe.

Visualize a happy yellow color. Allow this brilliant yellow to enter into your solar plexus, the area just below your ribs. Let its light outshine the darkness caused by constant ego demands. Allow the yellow light of true personal power to fill your solar plexus with its confidence and contentment. Know that you are good enough, bright enough, worthy enough to attain your needs and desires. Feel the clear, personal power of yellow moving now through your body and out into the world. You are the light!

Imagine a brilliant emerald green color beginning to circulate in your heart area. This green is of healing and of unconditional love. Allow darkness associated with jealousy, resentment, and anger to leave this area. Send the green into every cell in your body and love each cell, tissue, organ, and system. Tell your body that you love it and release it now from fear and worry. Tell your mind that love transcends all and that you now resolve to replace negativity and fear with love. Allow this brilliant emerald green to flow through your body and out into the world, healing and loving all that you encounter. You are love.

Imagine a brilliant blue light flowing in and through your throat. This is the color of communication. Make this little blue light bigger and brighter. Allow yourself to open the blue lines of communication, within and without. Listen for the voice of your Higher Self. Open now brilliant, blue lines of communication to that part that oversees your life and can guide you on the path of true love, and joy, and peace.

Imagine an indigo light in your forehead, between your eyes. Feel the presence of this deep color of wisdom and knowledge manifesting in your being. You can call upon this wisdom to assist you in making decisions, in determining right action, and in following your destiny. Allow this indigo wisdom to flow through every cell and atom of your body, and outward into your environment, to comfort and enlighten those around you as you move steadily upon the path of your Soul.

The clear violet light of transformation now flows in through the top of your head. Transformation of illness into wellness, of sadness into joy, of failure into success, and of anger and resentment into love. Allow this violet now to flow through your entire being, circulating into any remaining dark areas, cleansing and renewing your entire being.

When you look at a rainbow, you see all the colors in perfect balance. By closing your eyes slightly, you can see the colors merging together and yourself becoming surrounded by a pure white glow. This white light of spirit contains all colors and is indeed their source. Your Source is Spirit, God, Goddess, All That Is. All these colors are being supplied to you all the time. It is your choice how to use them. Commit now to renewing their brilliance each moment, each day.

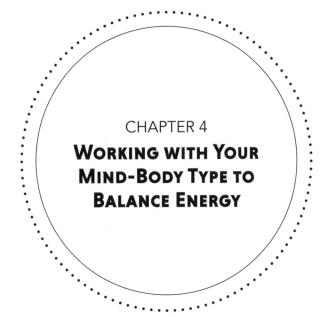

CHAPTER 4

WORKING WITH YOUR MIND-BODY TYPE TO BALANCE ENERGY

Here you will discover the concepts and tools you need to begin to view energy, nutrition, and exercise from a completely different perspective. This new perspective began with osteopathic physician Dr. Randolph Stone (1890–1981) and his desire to synthesize Western medicine with the Eastern traditional wisdom of Ayurveda.[41] Ayurvedic medicine is a holistic and preventative health care approach that has been used in India for over five thousand years and views the mind-body in terms of elements of nature and their combination in *doshas*.[42] *Vatta dosha* represents the elements of space and air. *Pitta dosha* represents water and fire. *Kapha dosha* represents water and earth. Well-being depends on the health of these doshas, which in turn depend on the health of the elements.

....

41. Associate Polarity Practitioner Class of 2010, "Digital Dr. Stone," Digital Dr. Stone Project, Colorado School of Energy Studies, accessed January 19, 2022, http://digitaldrstone.org/.
42. "Ayurveda," Healthwise, last modified September 23, 2020, https://www.uofmhealth.org /health-library/aa116840spec#.

Dr. Stone went directly to the five elements of the doshas in his work. In addition, Dr. Stone looked at the role of the body's electromagnetism in directing the five elements' flows. Every cell and organ in the human body has its own biomagnetic field.[43] Even the earth has its own electromagnetic field or frequency. Polarity therapy uses the knowledge of the body's biomagnetic fields to influence and unblock the natural flow of the energy fields of the five elements through the body. Polarity therapy is a comprehensive system of balancing these body-mind-spirit energies through hands-on energy balancing, nutrition, exercise, visualization, sound, reflexes, and counseling to promote well-being.

The foundation of Dr. Stone's work, and of polarity energy balancing is, in his own words, this: "'Life governs structure; structure limits life.' Life flows from within outward, and from above downward. The superior positive pole rules the inferior negative one by current flow. Disease is not an entity nor a fixed thing; it is nothing but a blockage of the currents of life in their flow and pattern circuits."[44] I chose to discuss polarity here because I trust the theory and use it as my main treatment modality. The source of much of this information comes from my training as a Certified Associate Polarity Practitioner.

It is not my intent or ability to train or certify polarity practitioners in this book. However, it is part of my practice to educate my clients on the techniques and practices that they may perform on their own to enhance their own and others' well-being. And I am honored to share this with you, my reader.

To begin, you'll complete a polarity self-assessment. From the insight you gain there, you'll be able to keep in mind the element of your highest score as you continue exploring polarity balancing. Along the way, you may find ways to bring into balance any areas in your body-mind-spirit that are currently unbalanced. Most of all, experiment with the suggested activities, and enjoy.

....

43. William Pawluk, "Understanding Natural and Therapeutic Magnetic Fields," Dr. Pawluk, accessed January 19, 2022, https://www.drpawluk.com/education/magnetic-science/biomagnetic-fields/.

44. Randolph Stone, *Health Building: The Conscious Art of Living Well* (Summertown, TN: CRCS Wellness Books, 1985), 184.

Practice
Polarity Energy and Five-Element Self-Assessment

Check all the boxes that apply and record the total number that you checked at the end of each section.

Ether Element	Air Element	Fire Element	Water Element	Earth Element
Sign	* Gemini * Libra * Aquarius	* Aries * Leo * Sagittarius	* Cancer * Scorpio * Pisces	* Taurus * Virgo * Capricorn
❑ Sinus congestion ❑ Breathing difficulties ❑ Abdominal problems ❑ Joint problems ❑ Throat problems ❑ Inability to express oneself ❑ Hearing problems, including ringing in the ears, tinnitus, and hearing loss	❑ Shallow breathing ❑ Tension in chest, locked scapulae ❑ Heart problems ❑ Shoulder or arm problems ❑ All nervous system problems ❑ Gas in abdominal area, flatulence, and bloating ❑ Pain, especially headaches, neck pain, and muscle spasm ❑ Exhaustion ❑ Arms feeling numb ❑ Radiating pain, neuralgia	❑ Sleep disturbances ❑ Immune system difficulties ❑ Stomach ulcers ❑ Liver problems ❑ Digestive problems ❑ Skin problems, including rashes, spots, and acne ❑ Smoking or drinking alcohol ❑ Migraine headaches ❑ Eye problems and disturbed vision ❑ Overanxious or constantly worried	❑ Breast lumps or tenderness ❑ Herpes ❑ Menstrual problems ❑ Prostate problems ❑ Foot problems ❑ Pelvic and lower back problems ❑ Skin problems with fire element ❑ Allergies	❑ Osteoporosis ❑ Diarrhea ❑ Constipation ❑ Colitis ❑ Spastic colon ❑ Hemorrhoids ❑ Chronic tension in neck, abdomen, or knees
Ether Element Total: _____	*Air Element Total:* _____	*Fire Element Total:* _____	*Water Element Total:* _____	*Earth Element Total:* _____

Polarity Therapy and the Five Elements

Who are you? In your essence, you are Spirit—eternal, infinite, and universal. When Spirit enters a body, the energy becomes denser as it binds itself to the earth plane. The energy of Spirit appears as streams of consciousness. Five thousand years ago, in India they were named ether, air, fire, water, and earth and became the basis for Ayurvedic health care.[45] One or more of these streams, elements, is dominant in us today.

Think about the last time you were with a group and see if you can recognize each element in action. Consider this example: Sue sat quietly, observing, above it all. Someone called her spacey. Her ether element was strong! Joe was quick and alert. He came up with lots of ideas. A great inspiration to others, but most of the time he was just full of air. Jack was a go-getter, risk taker, and liked being boss. He suggested many creative projects. Sometimes quick tempered, direct, and aggressive, Jack burned with the fire of inner creativity. Mary used her deep, intuitive, emotional senses to tell everyone how she, and they, felt. Her water element focused on the emotions of the group. Sam came up with practical ways to accomplish all the ideas of others. He was solid, dependable, and down-to-earth. We need all five of these personalities blended and in balance, in order to accomplish our goals in life.

Overview

In polarity therapy theory the soul or spirit, as a unit, receives its fine energy from an Inner Source or Inner Sun. Matter is the pole at the most remote distance away from the source of energy. As the vibrations of energy slow down, they crystallize, producing matter. Mind is the mediator of function between spirit and matter. Mind is healthy and functioning properly when it is ruled by the Soul or Spirit. But when mind is ruled by the senses, then matter predominates and peace leaves.

The five elements of polarity therapy—ether, air, fire, water, and earth—are present in everything that exists on the earth plane. Everything is created from them. The difference in life forms is the difference between which element is the most influential. In plants, the water element is the most influential.

....

45. "Ayurveda," Healthwise, last modified September 23, 2020, https://www.uofmhealth.org /health-library/aa116840spec#.

Only in human beings are all five present in equal balance. This fifth element, ether, represents the choice of right and wrong. It allows the spiritual chakras to open and provide access to higher realization. Each of the elements is represented in the lower five chakras and has the other four elements in them. For example, 50 percent of ether is ether and the other 50 percent is divided among the other four elements. The same ratios hold true for each of the lower five chakras. Polarity theory holds that there is constant change on the physical plane because the relationship of the five elements is constantly shifting. The elements originate on the causal plane—they are subtle mind energy. But the elements are unstable because they are antagonistic to each other. For example, too much water puts out fire, and too little water dries up the earth. Too much air causes a wildfire, while too little air makes fire impossible. Each element is constantly interacting with all others. This instability creates change, the cycles in life, day and night, the seasons, the stages of life, ups and downs, creation and expansion, crystallization, and death. It is only upon the death of the physical body that the elements return to their own essence.

The elements referred to in Ayurveda and in polarity therapy are not the same as the elements later in this book when we talk about feng shui. Ayurveda lineage is from India, while feng shui is Chinese in origin. Though there are some similarities, the way the elements are named and viewed are different. Here, in this chapter, we are talking about a succession of energy or vibrations from least dense to densest. This elemental energy begins to manifest physical form as ether element governing our mental processes. The air element, governing breath and movement, is a denser version of ether. Fire is a still denser, slower frequency than air and governs metabolism. Fourth is the water element dealing with bodily fluids, and fifth is the densest element, earth, which governs bones and dense organs.

It is time for an overview of each element.

The Five Elements and Your Mind-Body Type

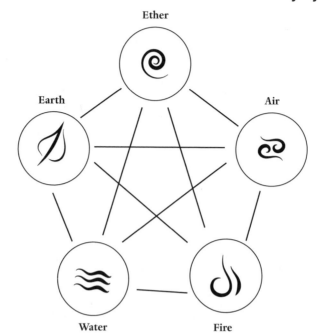

Ether

Earth

Air

Water

Fire

The Five Elements of Polarity

Ether: Ether is the prime element latent in all things, providing space and balance for all elements to unfold. Ether is essential to our sense of connectedness with spirit and well-being. In the body, ether is space, particularly in the chest and joints. Out of balance, we have problems with our breathing, joint pain, and difficulties expressing ourselves. Balanced ether promotes our sense of joy and union. Ether governs the spaces within the body, and disturbances appear most often as joint problems. Lack of ether is connected with the feeling of grief and separateness.

Air: Air is lightness and movement. On a still day we feel listless and heavy, while on a windy day we feel refreshed and enlivened. Air is associated with the east, a new day, and new beginnings. Air signs include Gemini, associated with the shoulders, arms, lungs, and respiration; Libra, associated with the kidneys; and Aquarius, associated with the legs. Imbalances are seen as nervous exhaustion, panic attacks, head-aches, gas, bronchitis, heart problems, neuralgia, and leg cramps. Air rules movement within the body and is associated with functioning of the lungs, heart, and nervous system. Balanced air promotes our senses of love, devotion, and compassion.

Fire: Fire is light and heat. Fire is transformative and is associated with willpower and creative force. Fire is connected with the south, the summer, and purification. Fire signs include Aries, associated with the head; Leo, associated with the solar plexus; and Sagittarius, associated with the thighs. Fire provides the heat for digestion and body tem-perature. Fire imbalances include headaches, eye disorders, digestive disorders, liver problems, pain, and weakness of the legs. Too much fire results in sympathetic dominance or the typical type A personal-ity, stressed and burned out! Unbalanced fire manifests as anger and resentment. Well-balanced fire is forgiveness and enthusiasm.

Water: Water is the source of all life, formless and flowing. Water is associated with the west, fall, and the time to go deep and let our emo-tions flow. Water signs include Cancer, associated with the breasts; Scorpio, associated with the genitals; and Pisces, associated with the feet. Water is associated with the genital and reproductive areas of the body, and body liquids. Imbalances may show as breast tenderness and lumps; skin, menstrual, prostate problems; and foot and back pain. Balanced water allows us to relax and let go, while imbalance reflects our attachment to worldly things.

Earth: Earth is dense, passive, the great provider. It has permanency and stability. Earth is associated with the north, winter, and material affairs. Earth signs include Taurus, associated with the neck; Virgo, associated with the bowels; and Capricorn, associated with the knees. The earth element rules the bones. Balanced earth reflects in strong bones, active assimilation and elimination, and flexible necks. When it is unbalanced, fear takes over and we experience neck stiffness, consti-pation, and weak bones (osteoporosis). Balanced, we find courage and contentment.

Knowing what each of five fields encompass is important to knowing what energies to apply where. For example, anger is too much fire. How do you calm fire? You can put water on it and create steam. You can put earth on it and bury it. You can withdraw air and put it out. On the other side of the coin, a person who is lethargic and depressed may have too little fire. In that case we can add more air to get the fire going or reduce water to allow drier conditions for the fire to burn. Polarity therapy requires problem-solving at its highest because each element must work in harmony with the other four elements. I enjoy the different combinations we can make for successful outcomes.

How the Elements and Polarity Come Together

The elements travel through the body in biomagnetic waves, going from positive (+) through neutral (o) to negative (–) poles. Ether, being a neutral element, does not have biomagnetic poles. Air polarizes in the shoulder (+), kidneys (o), and calves (–). Fire in the head (+), solar plexus (o), and thighs (–). Water includes the breasts (+), pelvis (o), and feet (–). Earth poles are neck (+), bowels (o), and knees (–). Polarity works to unblock stuck flows by connecting the energy between each pole. The energy is directed by placing both hands on the body, either front and back, side to side, or up and down.

As the energy flows between our right hand and our left hand, our own body energy (and the energy of another if we are using polarity on someone else) entrains to the movement of energy between our hands. We are not putting something into another person or taking something out of another. The movement of the energy between our hands allows the body to understand the direction to flow. The energy in the body part comes in resonance with the energy flowing between our hands. Working our way through areas of energy holding or deficit, we can help re-establish a normal flow. Similar to cleaning a gutter of leaves, once the flow is cleared, the body's own self-healing functions freely.

Practice
Self-Healing Activities

In the following sections we'll look at each element individually and how you can bring it into balance. Here are a couple of initial practices to ease you into the more specific practices to come.

Using Imagination
Use your imagination to bring elements into balance. For example, to cool a hot head, imagine floating in water. Generate new ideas by letting them soar in the clouds, and then ground them by planting idea seeds deep in the earth.

Using Your Hands
In these practices for self-healing, you will be using your hands. The energy of the elements runs through our fingers and toes. By holding and massaging a particular finger or toe, we can balance individual currents and flows within the entire body. Your right hand is your positive or giving hand. Your left hand is your negative or receiving hand. By placing your hands on your body opposite each other, front to back, side to side, or top to bottom, you automatically establish an energy flow between the positive and negative poles. For example, you could draw out inflammation by placing your left hand over the area and your right hand beside it. You could relax tight areas by placing your right hand over them and your left hand under to move the energy that has been stuck.

A headache located in your forehead, too much fire, may be relieved by placing your right hand on your forehead and your left hand down over your belly, sending the excess energy down into the pelvis to be cooled by the water element. The principle here is to remember that energy always moves from your right hand into your left hand. By your hand placement, you are creating a channel to direct the flow of biomagnetic energy. When an area feels too full, placing the right hand over that area and the left hand at a distance will allow the energy to drain off toward the left hand. When an area feels too empty, placing the left hand over it and the right hand at a distance sets up a flow of energy toward the left hand and the empty space. The terms *full* and *empty* are fairly easy to use. Place either hand over a place on your body and ask yourself, "Does this feel full or empty?" Your body will talk to you in your mind and give you an immediate answer. Then go from there.

Ether Element

Ether Element: Emotions

Sense: Hearing

Function: Expression, space

Body System: Space within the body, notably joints

Emotions: Return to spirit versus grief

Polarity Points: Above and below each joint

Polarity Reflexology: Big toe and thumb are neutral

Foods: Meditation

Visualization: Imagine infinite space, the galaxies, and bring that space into your body.

Sound: Aaaaaaaaa

Biomagnetic Polarities: Connect entrained energy above and below each joint using the thumb of the right hand below each joint and the middle finger of the left hand above each joint. The head is positive, the trunk is neutral, and the feet are negative.

The ether element is the source or field from which all other elements arise. Dr. Stone referred to ether as "the one river of life, flowing out of Paradise, which splits into four rivers of energy in the body, and waters and supplies it just as the rivers do the earth."[46] Least dense of all the elements, ether creates a unified field of subtle space for the movement of the other elements into physical form. The basic qualities of ether are stillness, harmony, and balance. It is the closest element in quality to the neutral center, or Source, and is the ground for manifestation of the mind-body complex. Ether is associated with the throat chakra.

In essence, ether is the space in which everything happens. A person who feels pressured has their ether out of balance. Ether in balance allows you to do everything with ease and without a sense of rushing or crowding.

Ether and the Emotions

Ether governs the mind and emotions and combines with other elements to create various qualities of emotion.

An element is considered "in" something when it combines with itself and another element. In the Western world we are used to looking at things as being separate: the head is separate from the neck. Elements in polarity theory are considered constantly combining with each other in a flow or dance. When ether is viewed alone, it is considered ether in ether and governs the emotional scale of grief to joy. When either is combined with air, ether in air, the emotional range of envy and desire to compassion and love are experienced. When either is combined with fire, ether in fire, emotions from anger and resentment to forgiveness and enthusiasm are experienced. When it combines with water, ether in water, the emotional range from attachment to letting go is experienced, and when ether combines with earth, ether in earth, the emotions of fear to courage are experienced.

Ether and the Body

In polarity, every joint is a neutral point of harmony, balance, a sense of going back to the source. Ether energy crosses over every joint, providing the space for movement. Ether also provides the space for movement within all body cavities and even within the body cells themselves. All body functions require space in which to perform. A tightening of space signifies lack of ether, while a feeling of spaciousness indicates too much predominance of ether with respect to other elements. Knowing this provides clues when energy balancing the ether element.

....

46. Randolph Stone, *Polarity Therapy: The Complete Collected Works*, vol. 2 (Summertown, TN: CRCS Wellness Books, 1986), book 4, 8.

Ether and Dis-ease

The medical profession currently diagnoses a disease by placing a label on a complex set of physical signs and symptoms. This label encapsulates the problem and places it in a category in which mechanical and chemical means may be used to resolve the problem. Polarity therapy recognizes areas of "dis-ease," areas where energy is not flowing smoothly. Dr. Stone believed that causes are always found in the energy field, never in matter.[47] Polarity therapy theory considers causes to be in the energy field first, not matter first. This theory is consistent with today's understandings of frequency and vibration. Energy is a blueprint for the physical. It's easier to change the blueprint before the building is built or go back and modify the blueprint before tearing down the structure. Lack of flow in the energy field may well invite dis-ease; however, it is a simple matter to encourage the energy to return to its natural, healthy state of flow. With this in mind, I now list potential dis-ease associated with the ether element.

Problems in the following areas may indicate an imbalance of the ether energies.

- Sinus congestion
- Breathing difficulties
- Abdominal problems
- Joint problems
- Throat problems
- Inability to express oneself
- Hearing problems, including ringing in the ears, tinnitus, and hearing loss

....

47. Stone, *Polarity Therapy*, vol. 2, book 1, 24.

Practice
Balance Ether

Ether is the most essential, purest, most perfect element latent in all things. It is intangible, the fundamental space out of which all other elements occur. So how does one go about balancing this elusive element?

Using Hand Polarity

Think of the energy in your hands. Your thumbs are ether energy as well as your big toes. Just as your left hand is a negative (receptive) charge, and your right hand is a positive (giving) charge, so each thumb and finger have a charge. To encourage the flow of ether over a particular joint, place the thumb of your right hand below the joint and the middle finger of your left hand above the joint. Gently allow the energy to flow across the joint space. You may also activate ether energy by making a fist with one hand and gently holding the thumb of your other hand inside. This sends energy to balance ether, the spleen and stomach, and worry.

Ether has a neutral thumb and big toe, so if you want to just give energy to a place on the body without moving it anywhere, use your thumb opposite your right index finger. To take away energy, place your thumb opposite your middle finger.

Too Much Ether

If you are feeling particularly spacey, as if there is too much energy in your head and none moving down below, try this technique. Place your right palm on the top of your head, then do the following:

1. Place your left index finger between your eyebrows and connect the energy, feeling it begin to flow downward.

2. Move your left index finger to the tip of your nose and connect the energy.

3. Place all your left fingertips on the middle of your sternum and massage gently. Feel the energy moving downward.

4. Move your left hand to the base of the sternum and hold gently directly over the solar plexus.

5. Place your left fingertips over the top of the pubic bone.

Numbers 1 through 5 are performed while holding your right palm on the top of your head. Finally, leave your left hand on the top of your pubic bone and move the right hand from the top of your head to the base of your spine at the coccyx. Hold both positions gently until your feel the flow of energy going down your legs and out your feet.

Too Little Ether

If you want to run the ether energy up instead of down, use a variation of the space button.[48] Sit on your right hand by placing your right fingertips at the junction between the coccyx and the sacrum, the hard bony area at the base of the lower back. Place two fingertips of your left hand on the mustache area between the upper lip and nose. Massage gently with the two upper fingers and then hold. Breathe deeply and imagine a movement of energy up the back and over the top of your head to the mustache area. Stop when you feel complete.

Visualization

Close your eyes and think about each of your joints, one at a time. Start with your toes. Visualize the joints in your toes being flexible and the joints moving freely. Move up to the bones in your feet and notice how flexible your feet are just by thinking about them. Move up to your ankles joints and see them strong and youthful. Now the knees and hips, visualizing the cartilage as smooth and the spaces in the joints open and flexible. Move up the bones of

....

48. John Chitty and Mary Louise Muller, *Energy Exercises: Easy Exercises for Health and Vitality* (Boulder, CO: Polarity Press, 1990), 75.

the spine, from your pelvis to your neck, seeing the joints between each vertebra open and spacious, allowing the nerves to exit the spinal cord freely. Now move down your neck to your shoulders and visualize your shoulder joints working freely. Move down to your elbows, wrists, hands, and fingers. See all your joints moving freely. Come back to your trunk and see how spacious it is between your organs, how much space is in your lungs for breath to enter and exit, and finally, how spacious your brain is, with the fluids flowing freely. Last, move out of your body and see the ether element extending back through time and space, feeding the body with energy. Open your eyes and feel how much space you have!

Sounds

Each element is associated with a particular sound. Vowel sounds can balance the elements. Say or sing "Aaaaaaa" to expand ether and create more space in your life. Try at first for one minute of Aaaaaaas.

Balanced ether results in a return to Spirit. And a return to Spirit balances ether. Any meditative techniques will work well for this balance. Periods of quiet in which you follow your own energy back into the quiet core of your being will open and expand the ether element in your body. Body follows mind. Think space … Think balance … Think stillness … Think harmony. And after thinking them, feel them. Feel space … Feel balance … Feel stillness … Feel harmony. Feel your way into the spaciousness of ether.

Air Element

Air Element: Movement
Sense: Touching
Function: Movement, expansion, diversity
Body Systems: Respiratory, nervous, circulatory
Emotions: Compassion, charity, love versus greed, and judgment
Polarity Points: Shoulders (+), mid-back and adrenals (0), calves (-)
Polarity Reflexology: Index finger and second toe are both negative (-)
Foods: Highest above ground, fruits, nuts, citrus
Visualizations: Feel the breath as it flows in and out of your nose
Sound: Eeeeee
Sight: Color green
Exercise: Stretch and move your shoulder blades up and down, forward and backward, side to side

Air is the wind and is associated with movement. Associated with the heart chakra, air reflects our lightness and ease of movement. Like the wind, air is pervasive and only perceptible when it moves. Like the wind, air is change-able. On a still day we feel listless and heavy, while on a windy day we feel refreshed and enlivened. Air is the medium for carrying things. Externally, it carries seeds, birds, sounds, while internally, it carries energy and motion. The air element is associated with the east, manifestation, the dawning of the day, new beginnings, and things coming into being. Air is movement and life!

In essence, air is the movement of all things within the space of ether. A person who feels pressured to rush around all the time, to have to move quickly, has their air out of balance. Air in balance allows free and relaxed motion, a sense of ease and flow.

Air and Movement

Air is associated with the five forms of movement in the body. Speed reflects air in air. A person who can't slow down, one who can't speed up, or one who is scattered reflects an air in air imbalance. Stretching is ether in air. One may stretch either physically or mentally! Shaking is fire in air. Trembling, uncertainty, and indecisiveness indicate a need for grounding. Flowing reflects water in air. A sense of all movement flowing, all words in rhythm and harmony, a mental flow. Contracting is earth in air. Too much earth may manifest as a tightening, a closing off on every level. Knowing this provides clues when energy balancing the air element.

Air and the Body

Air has its positive pole in the shoulders, ruled by Gemini; its neutral pole in the kidneys and adrenals, ruled by Libra; and its negative pole in the calves and ankles, ruled by Aquarius. The shoulders have been called the wings of life. When the shoulders are rigid and tight, the air element is congested in its positive pole, not flowing downward. Air also governs three major body systems: the respiratory system, the nervous system, and the circulatory system. In my practice of polarity therapy, air is the most common element to be out of balance. We stop circulating. Stress stimulates the adrenals and simultaneously tenses the shoulders. Our energy becomes locked in the upper body, and we are unable to ground and flow.

Air and Dis-ease

Problems in the following areas may indicate an imbalance of the air energies.

- Shallow breathing
- Tension in the chest, locked shoulder blades
- Heart problems
- Shoulder and arm problems
- All nervous system problems
- Gas in the abdominal area (flatulence and bloating)
- Pain, especially headaches, neck pain, and muscle spasms
- Exhaustion
- Arms feeling numb
- Radiating pain, neuralgias

Practice
Balance Air

The air element governs all movement in the body, from breathing to the transmission of impulses along the nerves to the beating of the heart and movement of blood through the arteries and veins. In addition, the air element governs the kidneys and adrenal glands. In today's modern world of stresses, it is more important than ever to keep the air element in balance.

Massage Fingers and Toes

The air element is associated with the negative, receiving energy of the index finger and second toe. A very simple way to encourage the flow of air is to massage these digits. A friend of mind was experiencing some of the dis-eases listed for air and called me on the phone. I asked her to check out her second toe on both feet. "Wow," she said when she returned to the phone. "My right second toe is flexible, but my left is like concrete—it's really solid!" She was experiencing most of her dis-ease on the left side of her body. She began a diligent program of toe massage, and the symptoms cleared.

Shoulder Stretch

An excellent exercise to mobilize the flow of air in the shoulder area is called the cliffhanger.[49] Stand with your back to a sturdy table, countertop, or back of a chair. Place the heels of your hands slightly behind you on the supporting surface. Now gently slide your bottom straight down toward the floor, allowing your hands to receive the weight of your body. Feel your shoulder blades stretching and moving closer together. Maintain this position without strain for several seconds, and then slowly stand up. This exercise is great to do hourly if you work at a desk or computer.

....

49. Stone, *Health Building*, 181.

Using Hand Polarity

Remember the polarity of your hands mentioned earlier. Your left hand is a negative, receptive charge, while your right hand is a positive, giving charge. You can connect the poles of air on your body simply by using your hands. Place one hand on your shoulder and the other hand on your low back/kidney area. Gently massage your shoulder and feel the energy begin to open and flow between shoulder and low back. Now move one hand down to your calf, while keeping the other on your low back. Massage your calf area and feel the energy flowing between calf and low back. To flow energy downward, use your left hand as the bottom one, keeping it closer to your feet than your right hand. To flow energy upward, use your left hand at the top, keeping it closer to your head than your right hand. Remember, energy flows from positive to negative, from your positive, giving right hand to your negative, receiving left hand.

Air is also the negatively charged index finger and second toe. To work with moving air on smaller areas, place the index finger on one side and the middle, positively charged finger on the opposite side. When working on the neck, place the middle finger on a sore spot indicating too much energy and the index finger on the opposite side of the neck. This will encourage the body to match the flow of energy from the middle finger to the index finger, from negative to positive, and relieve blocked energy at the sore spot. When doing this, remember that you are moving energy, not massaging the neck. Keep your fingers still and allow the energy to flow.

Visualization

The air element is powerful and controls three major systems (circulatory, nervous, and respiratory), and it's important to keep the element balanced and circulating throughout our energy mindbody. The easiest way to boost the air element is not a visualization; rather, it is an alternate nostril breathing technique from Ayurveda practices.[50] Sit, close your mouth, and then close your right nostril with your right thumb. Breathe naturally in and out through your left nostril eleven times. Now change and close your left nostril with your left thumb. Breathe in and out through your right nostril eleven times. With either hand, place your thumb over one nostril and your middle finger over the other. Alternate breathing between nostrils by opening and closing each side with your thumb and finger eleven times. Do not strain. If you find your nostrils are chronically clogged, you may choose to use a neti pot to cleanse them with warm salted water as part of your health routine.

Sounds

Each element is associated with a particular sound. Vowel sounds can balance the elements. Say or sing "Eeeeee" while feeling the air move in your chest.

When feeling low and lethargic, energize yourself by singing "Eeeeee" for at least sixty seconds. Air invigorates water and fans fire.

Balanced air allows you to open the heart chakra and flow with the universal force of Love in your life. With shoulders relaxed, breath deep, and heart open, you can meet any circumstance with flexibility. Change occurs. It really does! When we meet change with resistance and fear, we contract and temporarily lose this wonderful movement of air. Relax and greet the winds of change in your life. They are bringing you movement and growth.

....

50. Melissa Eisler, "Nadi Shodhana: How to Practice Alternate Nostril Breathing," Chopra, November 4, 2015, https://chopra.com/articles/nadi-shodhana-how-to-practice-alternate -nostril-breathing.

Fire Element

ð)

Fire Element: Metabolism

Sense: Seeing

Function: Motivation, will, drive, upward flow

Body Systems: Metabolism and digestion

Emotions: Forgiveness and enthusiasm versus anger and resentment

Polarity Points: From forehead (+) through solar plexus (o) to thighs (-)

Polarity Reflexology: Middle finger and middle toe are both positive

Foods: Foods next to the ground, including seeds, corn, wheat, rice, and other grains

Visualization: Imagine watching a blazing campfire and feel its warmth.

Sound: Iiiiiii

Sight: Look at the color yellow

Exercise: Stand and punch your fits out one at a time as if you were boxing. Shout HA with each punch.

The basic characteristics of fire are viewed as light, heat, and the sun. Fire can flare up and get easily out of control. We speak of a trial by fire as a cleansing and growing experience. Fire has the quality of transformation. Associated with the third chakra, the solar plexus, fire is the element of personal power, of willpower. Fire under control can provide heat, warmth, and protection. Fire is the third river of energy, which flows throughout the body-mind. Its strength or weakness affects all other elements in powerful ways.

Fire is the heat and light of all things. A fiery person gets things done, but often at the cost of harmony. Fire in balance is the power to accomplish our desires in our lives.

Fire and Metabolism

Fire is associated with the five aspects of metabolism in the body. Hunger is fire in fire. A fire in the belly, a hunger for the truth. Sleep is ether in fire. Too little ether will provide no space for fire to burn. This results in either sleeping too much or not being able to sleep at all. Thirst is air in fire. A thirst for knowledge, for information. Glow refers to the luster on the skin and represents water in fire. A healthy person has a bioluminescence, a quality of the skin that is absent in illness. Laziness, earth in fire, is literally doing nothing because the fire has been buried. Knowing this provides clues when energy balancing the fire element.

Fire and the Body

Fire has its positive pole in the head, ruled by Aries; its neutral pole in the solar plexus, ruled by Leo; and its negative pole in the thighs, ruled by Sagittarius. Headstrong people are usually fiery in nature. The intense, overbearing, demanding perfectionist reflects fire in the head. Anger and resentment, usually expressed in the form of ulcers, is too much fire in the belly. The liver is also considered an organ of fire. Problems with the liver may be seen in vision problems. Leg weakness often reflects a lack of downward flow of fire—it's all stuck up in the belly and repressed there. Fire circulating freely permits us to move through life in a positive and exciting way.

Fire and Dis-ease

Problems in the following areas may indicate an imbalance of the fire energies.

- Sleep disturbances
- Immune system difficulties
- Stomach ulcers
- Liver problems
- Digestive problems
- Skin problems, including rashes, spots, and acne
- Smoking or drinking alcohol
- Migraine headaches
- Eye problems and disturbed vision
- Overanxious or constantly worried

Practice
Balance Fire

The fire element is easily unbalanced by food, by emotions, by living life in society with others. Telling what went wrong is more common for many than telling what went right. When we complain to others about how bad the traffic, weather, or work was, we usually get an audience agreeing with us. But what happens if we tell people we are so excited about finding the perfect toothpaste or socks? There is less support and often we are considered bragging. Balanced fire is enthusiasm and often our society prefers anger to excitement and enthusiasm.

Massage Fingers and Toes

The fire element is associated with the positive, giving energy of the middle finger and third toe. A very simple way to encourage the flow of fire is to massage these digits. However, most of us have too much fire. Just look at a person who uses the middle finger in a gesture of anger! This is repressed and expressed fire in action. In this case, fire must be calmed rather than stimulated. Massaging the ring finger, the water finger, will literally put water on fire to calm it down.

Using Hand Polarity

Remember the polarity of your hands. Your left hand is a negative (receptive) charge, while your right hand is a positive, giving charge. You can connect the poles of fire on your body simply by using your hands. Placing one hand on your head in the area of the eyes and forehead and the other hand on your solar plexus/belly area is especially effective. Gently massage your belly and feel the energy begin to open and flow between it and your head. Now move one hand down to your thigh, while keeping the other on your belly. Massage each thigh one at a time and feel the energy flowing between thighs and belly. To flow energy downward, use your left hand as the bottom one, keeping it closer to your feet than your right hand. To flow energy upward, use your left hand at the top, keeping it closer to your head than your right hand. Remember, energy flows from positive to negative, from your positive, giving right hand to your negative, receiving left hand.

Fire is the positively charged middle finger and third toe. For specific point tenderness anywhere on the body, place the middle finger on the tender point and the index finger a distance away on the body. Energy will flow from your middle finger toward your index finger, drawing excess energy away from the tender point. For example, for a bruise on the front of the thigh, place your middle finger on the bruise and your index finger on the back of the thigh directly behind the bruised area. When doing this, remember that you are moving energy, not massaging the bruise. Keep your fingers still and allow the energy to flow.

Visualization: The Path of Fire

Fire is often suppressed in the belly area. We do not have a lot of opportunity to express this expansive energy. When angry, we cannot run around, scream, and shout. Our bosses or our families simply will not put up with it. And we often cannot express fire in a positive way—that is, by shouting for joy or performing vigorous exercise. You may find the following mental imagery useful for facilitating the flow of the current of fire within you. It is called the Path of Fire.

The fire element flows through a definite pathway within and around your body. Imagining this flow actually helps it move. As you perform the following imagery, note places where the fire seems easy to imagine and areas where it seems more difficult. The difficult areas indicate blocks that will resolve with gentle encouragement. Visualize a stream of energy coming in through the bottom of your left foot. Run this energy up your left leg and let it cross over from the left hip to the navel area. From the navel, take this energy up to the right shoulder, across the shoulder, and up the neck to your right ear. Let the energy cross over the top of your head and come down to the left ear. Now guide the energy down your neck and into your left shoulder. From here, take it down to your navel and across to your right hip. Now let the energy flow down your right leg and out the bottom of your right foot.[51]

The majority of people who perform this exercise notice a definite resistance to the downward flow of energy. It is easier to bring the energy up and into the head than it is to allow the energy to flow down and out the right foot. This is reflective of our inability to let go. We take in and hold on tight! One client of mine with sinus problems could not initially get the energy into the head. The flow went directly across the shoulders, thus cutting off the head entirely! With practice, the client was able to visualize the flow up over the head and down, and the sinus problems were greatly relieved.

Sounds

Each element is associated with a particular sound. Vowel sounds can balance the elements. Say or sing "Iiiiiii," feeling it, the sound of fire, in the solar plexus. Try to sing this for at least one minute.

When feeling out of balance, repeat the sound Iiiiiii to energize your fire and balance your air.

Balanced fire brings energy and vitality to life. It allows the action necessary for you to carry out your will. Fire brings a spark to your projects and relationships. It brings a twinkle to your eyes and a sense of excitement to your life. Fire under control provides protection and comfort. May you always have the fire of life burning brightly.

....

51. Stone, *Polarity Therapy*, vol. 1, book 3, 58.

Water Element

Water Element: Tasting
Sense: Tasting
Function: Creativity, sexuality, downward flow
Body System: Bodily fluids
Emotions: Letting go versus attachment
Polarity Points: From breasts (+) through pelvis (o) to feet (-)
Polarity Reflexology: The ring finger and fourth toe are both negative (-).
Foods: Foods that grow above ground or nearest to it, including vegetables, cucumbers, melons, tomatoes, strawberries; sea foods
Visualizations: Imagine floating on the ocean, feeling the waves rise and fall.
Sound: Ooooo
Sight: The color orange
Exercise: Lie on your stomach, bend your knees, and swing your legs back and forth in a scissor-like motion.

Water is formless, feminine, magical, and healing. The moon influences the tides. We begin in water in the womb, the source of life. Water is associated with purification and baptism. Depth of feeling, emotions, and the ability to let them flow are a part of water. A shape changer, water exists in different forms under different conditions. Water needs the help from other elements to move and is contained in and channels through other elements. Water is also a universal solvent, with abilities to dissolve materials. Located in the second chakra, water is associated with our relationships with others and ourselves.

Water is versatile and adaptable. It can change in response to varying conditions. A person with the water element dominant will go with the flow, use a light touch, and trust the process. They also may be viewed as being wishy-washy and unable to stand firm on their beliefs and decisions.

Water and Secretions

Water is associated with body secretions. Saliva is ether in water. Sweat is air in water. Urine is fire in water, while semen or vaginal fluid is water in water. Blood and lymph are earth in water. Disturbances in any of these areas indicate unbalanced proportions of water to the other elements. Knowing this provides clues when energy balancing the water element.

Water and the Body

Water has its positive pole in the breast and lymph areas, ruled by the sign of Cancer. Its neutral pole is in the genitals, ruled by Scorpio, and its negative pole is in the feet, ruled by Pisces. Watery people are easily able to go with the flow, sometimes resulting in taking a form imposed by someone else. Remember that water will conform to its container and change shape according to the temperature. The flow of water may be interrupted by both internal and external events. In nature, if water is contained in a pool without access to flow, it becomes stagnant. Air bubbling through water results in clarity and renewal. The water element in our bodies interacts with all other elements in profound ways.

Water and Dis-ease

Problems in the following areas may indicate an imbalance of the water energies.

- Breast lumps or tenderness
- Herpes
- Menstrual problems
- Prostate problems
- Foot problems
- Pelvic and lower back problems
- Skin problems in association with the fire element
- Over-sensitivity to touch
- Allergies

Practice
Balance Water

The water element is important to our emotional stability. The ability to let life happen, to go with the flow, to not fight the current are all metaphors for the water element in our lives. The practice of nonattachment to results is key here. The ability to do what we are called to do and then move on to the next piece of our lives reflects the water element. Water is nurturing and supportive when we allow it to be.

Massage Fingers and Toes

The water element is associated with the negative, receiving energy of the ring finger and fourth toe. A very simple way to encourage the flow of water is to massage these digits. Try it the next time you are feeling stagnant or confined and let the flow, flow!

Five-Pointed Star

Another technique that is useful for balancing the water element is called the five-pointed star. Sit or lie down in a comfortable position. Touch your left pelvic area with your right palm, and your right upper chest area with your left palm, fingertips touching your left shoulder. Gently rest both hands in this position until you feel complete. You may feel a sense of relaxation of muscles, a tingle of energy, or simply a feeling of satisfaction. Then move your upper hand to rest gently on your throat. This is the contact point for the top of the five-pointed star you are making on your torso. Again, wait for a sense of completion to occur. Now do the same contacts on the opposite hip and shoulder. Touch your right pelvic area with your left palm and your left shoulder area with your right palm. Wait for the relaxation to occur. Then place your right hand gently over your throat. Feel the energy beginning to move and flow. Finally, hug yourself by crossing your arms and placing your hands on opposite shoulders. Relax and feel the flow of the water element throughout your body. Feel water mixing with air to stimulate you, mixing with fire to calm you, and flowing into the space of ether. Feel the new balance and flow.[52]

Using Hand Polarity

Remember the polarity of your hands. Your left hand is a negative, receptive charge, while your right hand is a positive, giving charge. You can connect the poles of water element on your body simply by using your hands. Place one hand on your breast/upper chest area and the other hand on your lower abdominal/pelvic area. Gently massage your lower abdomen and feel the energy begin to open and flow between it and your chest. Now move one hand down to your pelvic area and bend your leg so that your foot comes into reach of your other hand. Massage your foot and feel the energy flowing between foot and pelvis. To flow energy downward, use your left hand as the bottom one, keeping it closer to your feet than your right hand. To flow energy upward, use your left hand at the top, keeping it closer to your head than your right hand. Remember, energy flows from positive to negative, from your positive, giving right hand to your negative, receiving left hand.

Water is the negatively charged ring finger and fourth toe. This finger can be used in place of the index finger when moving energy with your fingers because they are both negatively charged.

Visualization

The best visualizations for the water element are accompanied by the sound of water. Sleep machines often have tracks for ocean waves, rain, flowing creeks, and the sounds of waves lapping on the side of a boat. Listening to these sounds takes you to a place where the energy of water cools and soothes you. You may also simply close your eyes and imagine the last time you were at the

....

52. Chitty and Muller, *Energy Exercises*, 77.

beach or in a boat and go there in your mind. Water is all about letting go. Waves don't stay still; they come and go. Our lives don't stay still; they too come and go.

Sounds

Each element is associated with a particular sound. Vowel sounds can balance the elements. Say or sing the following sounds aloud, repeating each three times. Feel the water element by singing or chanting the vowel sound, "Ooooo." You may even feel its energy in your pelvis while chanting. Try to keep it up for at least one minute. Water invigorates air and calms fire.

Balanced water brings a sense of calmness and flow into your life. You are able to flow around obstacles or gently wear them down. You have a new sense of harmony and trust, as your deeper emotions flow toward the surface and become cleansed and renewed. Trust the process of flow in your life today.

Earth Element

Earth Element: Body Forms
Sense: Smelling
Function: Structure, crystallization
Body System: Skeletal, waste elimination
Emotions: Courage versus fear
Polarity Points: From neck (+) through bowels (o) to knees (−)
Polarity Reflexology: The little finger and little toe are both positive (+)
Foods: Foods that grow underground, including potatoes, beets, onions, garlic, and herbs; meat
Visualization: Imagine sitting on the ground in a deep forest.
Sound: Uuuuuuu
Sight: The color red
Exercise: Squat down, keeping knees behind toes with back and bottom down as if you were using a commode located in the floor and rock gently.

Earth is dense, passive, and fertile. Earth is the great provider, associated with permanency and stability. Earth provides shelter and protection. Earth provides clay, brick, wood, and food. Associated with the first or root chakra, the earth element provides the grounding necessary to exist on the physical plane. Earth also has the capacity for absorbing other elements in this manifestation process. Earthy people are down-to-earth, grounded, and solid. Place an earth person in the room with an air person and just watch what happens. The airy personality will be standing, pacing, circling around the earthy person, seated comfortably and just observing.

We need the quality of earth to ground our ideas and manifest our dreams. Earth brings our thoughts down to reality and provides a stable foundation for building our lives.

Earth and Form

Earth is associated with bodily forms. Hair is ether in earth, skin is air in earth, blood vessels are fire in earth, muscles are water in earth, and bones are earth in earth. Disturbances in any of these areas indicate unbalanced proportions of earth to the other elements. The common concern of osteoporosis with aging indicates a lack of the earth element. As we grow older, we are more active in our thoughts, ether in air, than with our bodies. Physical activities, especially in natural settings, increase the earth element regardless of age. Knowing this provides clues when energy balancing the earth element.

Earth and the Body

Earth has its positive pole in the neck area, ruled by the sign of Taurus. Its neutral pole is in the colon, ruled by Virgo, and its negative pole in the knees, ruled by Capricorn. Knees and bowels are common areas of concern with aging. Too much earth energy slows down the digestive system and clogs the space in the joints. Too little accounts for fragility of hair, skin, and bones. Gardening is a great way to increase earth energy easily. Being out in nature, feeling the earth through your fingertips, connects one with earth itself. Stretching, reaching, and bending loosen the joints and return flexibility and space to the body.

Earth and Dis-ease

Problems in the following areas may indicate an imbalance of the earth energies.

- Osteoporosis
- Constipation
- Colitis
- Spastic colon
- Hemorrhoids
- Chronic tension in the neck, abdomen, or knees

Practice
Balance Earth

Let's talk for a moment about grounding and how it is often lacking in today's world. Grounding occurs naturally when we garden, build, walk in nature, walk barefoot on the grass, lie on the ground, and sit under a tree. Unfortunately, many of us do not have that opportunity often. Living in high-rise apartment buildings, working in climate-controlled buildings, coming home and turning on the air-conditioning often results in an imbalance in the earth element.

Massage Fingers and Toes

The earth element is associated with the positive, giving, energy of the little finger and toe. A very simple way to encourage the flow of earth is to massage these digits. Use it to ground yourself when you are feeling spacey or out of it.

The Earth Button

Earth energy may be balanced easily by a technique known as the earth button.[53] Place two fingers of your left hand directly above the pubic bone and two fingers of your right hand just below the lower lip. Massage gently with the two upper fingers and then gently hold both contacts. Breathe deeply, visualizing the movement of energy down the center of your body. Look up and down with your eyes, without moving your head, to assist the top-bottom connection. When you feel the energy flow is complete, remove your hands from their contacts. Finish by looking around in a downward direction. Downward eye placement activates the top-bottom dimension of the brain. This emphasizes the feeling of stability and anchors in a feeling of being grounded.

....

53. Chitty and Muller, *Energy Exercises*, 75.

Using Hand Polarity

Remember the polarity of your hands. Your left hand is a negative, receptive charge, while your right hand is a positive, giving charge. You can connect the poles of the earth element on your body simply by using your hands. Place one hand on your neck and the other hand on your lower abdominal area. Gently massage your lower abdomen and feel the energy begin to open and flow between it and your neck. Now move one hand down to your abdominal area and place your other hand on your knee. Massage your knee and feel the energy flowing between knee and abdomen. To flow energy downward, use your left hand as the bottom one, keeping it closer to your feet than your right hand. To flow energy upward, use your left hand at the top, keeping it closer to your head than your right hand. Remember, energy flows from positive to negative, from your positive, giving right hand to your negative, receiving left hand.

Earth is the positively charged little finger and toe. This finger can be used in place of the middle finger when moving energy with your fingers because they are both positively charged.

Visualization

Visualize yourself having a hollow tail, a dragon tail, extending out from the base of your spine. Now send that tail down into the earth. Stretch your tail deeper and deeper into the earth, until your tail reaches the place of the most abundant earth energy possible. Now begin to bring the earth energy up through your tail and into your body through the base of your spine. Let that warm, thick earth energy move up your spinal column and out through your nerves, calming, warming, soothing. Feel the earth moving through your arms and legs, through your trunk, up into your neck and head. Everywhere the energy touches you are soothed and calmed. Gently open your eyes, feeling relaxed and grounded.

Sounds

Each element is associated with a particular sound. Vowel sounds can balance the elements. Say or sing "Uuuuuu" and feel the earth

energy deep at the base of your spine. When feeling out of balance, repeat the sound for one minute. Earth calms air and fire.
Use "Uuuuuu," for earth, during stressful activity to calm down.

Balanced earth brings a sense of grounding into your life. You are able to
turn your ideas into reality and see them take form. Time spent in nature, sitting on the ground, playing in the dirt, stimulates the earth energy. So take
a break and go hug a tree. Tell your boss, family, or friends that you are just
doing your therapy to balance your energy. Maybe they will even join you!

Practice
Additional Ways to Balance
the Five Polarity Elements

As mentioned earlier, polarity balancing combines visualization,
sound, and reflexes, which we've addressed as we looked at each
of the elements individually. We'll now look at some simple practices related to nutrition and exercise that you can do to balance
the five elements.

Nutrition

Food increases the flow and potency of elements. Air foods grow
high above the ground, including fruits and nuts. Seeds and grains
growing above the ground, like sesame and sunflower seed, corn,
wheat, rice, and beans, increase the fire of digestion. Water foods
grow nearest to the ground, like green vegetables and melons.
Balance a fiery system by adding a sense of flow to the body.
Comfort foods of earth grow under the ground, such as potatoes,
carrots, onions, and beets, and provide a sense of grounding and
stability.[54]

....

54. Stone, *Polarity Therapy*, vol. 2, 202–3.

Think back to your self-assessment quiz and which element appeared to be weakest. When you wish to strengthen an element, eat more of the foods that nourish it. For example, in the heat of summer we tend to eat more water foods—melons, cantaloupes, and so forth—to cool the summer heat and fire element. In the winter, to warm up and increase the fire element, we often consume more grains and breads. We naturally select the foods we need and can consciously reinforce these selections based on polarity theories.

The fun part of looking at the body's energies through polarity is in the creative problem-solving it invites. For example, regardless of the time of year, if a person is always angry or has problems with metabolism and digestion, we can look at the type of food they are eating. Chances are it is lots of wheat, rice, beans. There is a whole industry of gluten-free foods that tackle this problem. But what if all it took was to calm the fire and change the diet to more watery foods or fewer air foods? Viewing health issues through the frame of the five elements has the potential to resolve many problems naturally.

Practice
Balancing Polarity Exercises

A few basic exercises done daily for two to three minutes without stress or strain can balance the elements. Check with your medical adviser prior to beginning any new exercise program.

Chair Cliffhanger: The chair cliffhanger balances ether and air. Sit in a chair with armrests and place your hands upon the armrests. Push up on your hands, straightening your arms and lifting your buttocks off the chair. Keep your feet flat on the floor. Feel the stretch between your shoulder blades as the muscles gently lengthen and relax. Do not strain. Repeat two to three times.[55]

Punching: Punching balances fire. Stand with both hands in fists, take a breath, and push your right hand out forcibly while shouting, "Ha." Breathe in while punching your left hand out. Shout! Really release the pent-up fire that has been repressed inside.[56]

Scissor Kick: The scissor kick balances water. Lie on your stomach, bend your knees, and swing your lower legs back and forth across each other. Feel the muscles in your hips and pelvis begin to relax. Make the movements gentle and smooth. Just kick and relax![57]

Cerebral Spinal Bounce: The cerebral spinal bounce balances earth. Stand with your feet apart, hands on thighs, and arms straight. Bend the knees and gently bounce the body in rhythmical movement. You may rock back and forth or from side to side. Gently feel the flow of energy going downward, grounding through your feet into the earth below.[58]

Squat: The squat is used to bring all elements into balance. Bend your knees and squat down, with elbows at knees and hands holding the bottom of your feet. Gently rock while in this position. When performing this exercise, try to have your feet flat on the floor and your knees behind your toes. You may place a book under your heels at first to maintain this position without undue stress.[59]

Most of all, listen to your own body and do the exercises within your comfort zone.

....

55. Stone, *Health Building*, 179.
56. Angela Plum, basic APP training, Academy of Natural Therapies, Marshall, NC, 2000.
57. Stone, *Polarity Therapy*, vol. 1, book 2, 61.
58. Plum, basic APP training.
59. Stone, *Health Building*, 163.

All dis-ease is a by-product of an imbalanced energy system. Our energy becomes disorganized when we experience mental, emotional, or physical strain or trauma. When we play in the world of ego and become disconnected from Source. When we forget to love ourselves and love others. The good news is that energy can easily be realigned. Polarity, and other energy modalities, facilitate that alignment. Removing energy blocks is the first step. The next one is for each of us to decide to fully connect with the eternal source of energy, balance, and health.

Listen to your body and feel the flow of energy. Notice times when you feel stiff and stagnant and bring in air and water. Notice the times when you feel hyper and spacey and bring in earth and fire. Notice your emotions and view them in terms of a disruption of the elements and not as caused by something outside yourself. Then use polarity, meditation, and chakra energies to help you realign. May you be well.

Integrations

Now that we've looked at meditation, chakras, and five-element energy balancing, it's time to use them for practical energy problems. When I treat a client in polarity therapy, they tell me first their medical diagnosis, migraine headaches, constipation, or a pain in the shoulder. I then reframe them into energy terms. The thing about energy is that it is different from conventional medicine. In conventional medicine if you have a headache, the focus will be on your head and brain. However, in energy medicine, the focus will be on how your energy is flowing through your entire body. That doesn't mean that we can't start where the symptoms are manifesting. If a rock is in a fishing net, maybe its easier to just pull the rock out first than try to correct all the stretching that is occurring at more distal points of the net.

With that said, the following are brief examples of the tools you may use for self-healing by body part. It's a good place to start as long as you remember that it's all connected!

Practice
Quick Energy Techniques by Body Location

Head

When feeling spacy or confused, ground yourself by bringing earth energy up to your head.

- Walk barefoot in nature.

- Look at your diet and eat more grounding foods. The neutral aspect of head energy is the stomach.

- Massage your thighs.

- Massage your little fingers, associated with earth.

Head

Feeling constricted or pressured, without enough space to think. Lighten up, running the energy stuck in your head down and out your feet.

- Go out and look at the night sky and meditate on the vast spaciousness of the universe.

- Eat lighter, higher foods.

- Massage your thumbs and big toes.

- Use a mantra meditation, a repeated sound to take you higher.

Throat

Feeling as if you have "lost your voice." Experiencing phlegm, hoarseness, tightness, or constriction in the throat and neck area.

- Sing! Sing a song. Sing a mantra. Sing a note ... Practice speaking your truth calmly, without drama. Exercise your neck. Look left and right, up and down. Tilt your ear to your shoulder. Circle your head counterclockwise, then clockwise. Do each motion slowly, with awareness and without pain.

- Stimulate and strengthen your knees through massage and exercise. Eat foods that help regulate your bowels. Massage your little finger and the little toes.

- Tone your voice by singing the vowel sounds or a mantra.

Heart and Lungs

Feelings of restriction in the chest area, closed rather than open, congested, heavy. (Note: these practices, as all practices in this book, are not a replacement for medical attention; instead, they call you to become aware of general feelings of lack of wellness in different body parts.)

- Move your shoulder blades up and down, backward and forward, in circles counterclockwise, and in circles clock-wise.

- Eat air foods: nuts and fruits that grow high above the earth. Massage the index fingers and the toe next to the big toe.

- Practice breath control. Breathe slowly and deeply to calm and expand the lungs and calm the nervous system, which will calm the heart.

Solar Plexus

Are you angry? Resentful? Fearful of others? Do you have any stomach ulcers or stomach problems?

- Calm the fire of anger with forgiveness. Forgive everyone and everything and forgive yourself over and over until you can feel the energy shift.

- See true self as a spiritual being, as lesson 97 of *A Course in Miracles* shares: "Spirit am I…free of all limits, safe and healed and whole, free to forgive and free to save the world."[60]

- Massage your ring finger or fourth toe (associated with the water element) or little finger or fifth toe (associated with the earth element) to calm the fire. Remind yourself that life is too good to be wrapped up in anger and fear. Find something that brings enthusiasm and do it.

Bowels and Generative Organs

Are you feeling "all bound up" with constipation or too flighty with diarrhea or just not comfortable in your own skin?

- Use affirmations: "Every day in every way I'm getting better and better." Send these areas positive thoughts and energy. Love them!

- Massage your ring and middle fingers to enliven them.

Legs

Feeling too tired to walk across the room, too much pain in your legs, or weak in your legs.

- Sit on the ground daily if you can.

- Walk barefoot in the morning dew.

- Imagine bringing earth energy up through your feet, your ankles, your calves, your knees, and your thighs. Allow that energy to continue to flow upward, filling your trunk, your chest your neck; flowing down your shoulders to your arms and hand; flowing up into your head; and finally flowing out the top of your head.

....

60. Helen Schucman, *A Course in Miracles* (New York: Foundation for Inner Peace, 1975), 89.

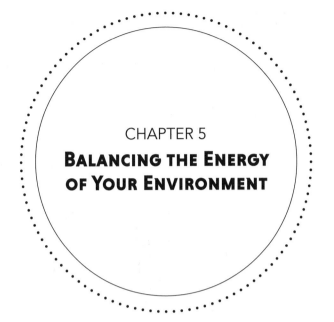

CHAPTER 5

BALANCING THE ENERGY OF YOUR ENVIRONMENT

Feng shui, pronounced *fung shway*, is the idea of living in harmony and balance with our environment and dates back between three and six thousand years ago, depending on the source.[61] It is the study of energy, chi, and how its circulation affects people. The circulation of these invisible energy frequencies can be blocked or distorted by our environment, thus creating negative energy, known as *shar chi*.

There are many different schools of feng shui in China. For example, the form school, which began in southern China with its varied landscape, studies the natural environment—mountains, lakes, and streams—and seeks to place buildings and dwellings in harmony with the landscape. The compass school originated in northern China's relatively flat landscape and relies on the cardinal directions for proper arrangement of a room, office, or home. This section

....

61. Tania Yeromiyan, "What Is Feng Shui: A Brief Guide," CLI, last modified August 9, 2021, https://studycli.org/chinese-culture/what-is-feng-shui/.

describes practical applications of the compass school in the placement of colors, symbols, and other auspicious objects according to the compass directions.

Basic Principles of Feng Shui

Feng shui is about being in harmony with nature and your environment. Many things we do, such as cleaning a room of clutter when we feel depressed, are feng shui tools. The idea of being in balance is often difficult for the Western mind to grasp.

The Balance of Yin and Yang

Yin-Yang Symbol

The concept of opposites in perfect balance is called yin and yang in the East. Yin and yang are opposites that are constantly evolving and cycling. In this balance are transformation, interaction, and interdependence. Look at the symbol of yin and yang for a moment. Within the dark, yin, is the light of yang. Within the light of yang is the dark of yin. Even the words *dark* and *light* have different meaning in terms of feng shui. Yin is the dark, night, negative, receiving force of energy associated with the moon, water, and feminine qualities. Yang is the sunny, light, positive, sending force of energy associated with fire, the summer, and masculine qualities. It is natural for winter to be the opposite of summer, for the day to follow the night. They give each other meaning and need each other to exist.

According to feng shui, the dance of opposites of yin and yang maintains the balance of the cosmos. We too, in our environments, require a balance of opposites. Imagine living in an all-white room with the lights on all the time. In this room the floor is white, all the furniture is white, and the light never ends. How long could you stay in such a room? An hour, a day, a week? With nothing to contrast, with nothing to stand out, what would your life be like? Now into this room add some yin. Turn off the lights at night. Add a black sofa and a black coffee table. The room improves because there is more contrast, and therefore more balance. Now add variations of color to the white and black. A green rug. Blue walls. Yellow flowers. Now the room becomes livable. Now you can feel at home.

Feng shui uses colors and textures and objects all designed to create a balance and harmony in any environment. When you bring your environment into harmony, you can flow your energies better. You can accomplish more with less stress. And you attract to you balance and harmony in affairs of your life.

As you read about the elements and cures and things to do to feng shui an area, please be gentle with yourself. All this information can be both exciting and overwhelming. It's exciting to know that some simple changes in your environment may relieve your stress and open your space to more positive energy. It will be overwhelming if you feel you must change everything and all at once. Original feng shui and some schools of feng shui today are rigid in their implementation of cures, saying that if you don't do a certain thing in a certain way, all hope is lost. My intent in including a chapter of feng shui is to open you to looking at the energy in your environment as well as the energy in yourself. If you do feng shui with anxiety and pressure, then that anxiety and pressure will be infused in whatever you do. Please take information on feng shui with a grain of salt. If something feels right, then do it. Feeling right means by doing it, you feel better and happier and have added to your well-being in some way. If not, you can read the suggestion and come back to it later. I hope you enjoy looking at your environment with the fresh eyes of feng shui.

Feng Shui Cures

Feng shui cures or remedies are objects in the environment that can shift energy when necessary to attain balance. As noted earlier, in feng shui, negative energy is called shar chi. Negative energy occurs when there are physical or emotional blocks to the flow of energy. For example, before we moved to the mountains, my husband and I lived in a hundred-year-old Southern farmhouse with windows everywhere and doors opening off every room, to catch the breeze on a hot summer day. There were very few blocks to energy flow in that old house. Our new house in the mountains lacked that old Southern flowing design. The rooms felt small and closed, with fewer windows and doors. We immediately went out and bought mirrors for each room. The mirrors opened the space and reflected the beautiful mountains inside. Without realizing it, we were using a feng shui cure. We had not even heard of the term *feng shui* at that time; we just knew that we needed to open the space.

You have probably used cures without knowing why. Most cures are a combination of common sense and good taste. There are eight basic cures in feng shui. These cures are used to generate energy when the structure of the room or building prevents an open energy flow. Feng shui cures include the use of the following:

Bright Objects: Mirrors, faceted crystal balls, gems, lights, and candles

Sounds: Wind chimes, bells, and music

Living Chi: Flowers, plants, birds, and fish

Moving: Mobiles, chimes, and fountains

Heavy: Stone sculptures and furniture

Mechanical: Computers, stereos, and TVs

Bamboo: Flutes

Color: Relates to each area on baqua map

The Baqua

In arranging an environment, nine areas are noted to be of special significance. These nine areas also reflect the major aspects of life. The *baqua*, or *bag'ua*, map shows the nine separate areas of energy and intention in feng shui. Baqua means "eight-sided" and is pictured as an octagonal shape. You may superimpose the map over any floor plan or any room of a home or office to see what areas need attention. This chapter provide basic information for using the map to improve the flow of energy in any environment.

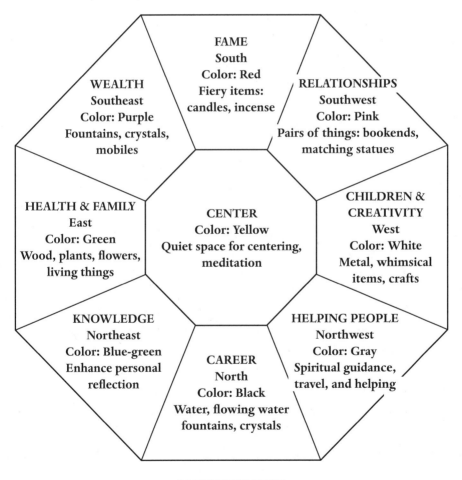

MAIN ENTRANCE

The Baqua Map

The Five Elements of Feng Shui

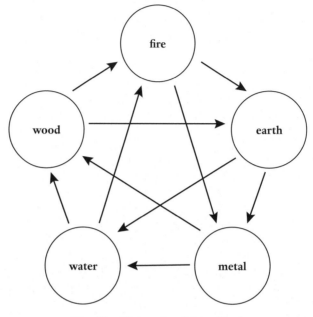

The Five Elements of Feng Shui

In the previous chapter we used the five elements of earth, air, fire, water, and ether to describe energy flows in the body based on Ayurvedic principles from ancient India. The five elements differ in feng shui, which is based on ancient Chinese teachings. Though some have similar names, they are used in a completely different context. I have made attempts to correlate the elements from the two different traditions with each other, and it is like matching apples with oranges. For example, the earth element in Ayurveda, and thus in polarity practice, represents grounding. In feng shui it represents centering. In performing energy work we are taught to ground and center. Two different concepts, one from India and the other from China. We ground using the energy of the root chakra and we center using the energy of feng shui. My best advice to you while reading this is to not twist your tail trying to match the two sets of five elements with each other. It's tempting to try to sort it out. It's more meaningful to understand another interpretation of energy and go with it for now.

The East: Health and Family

The east represents the area in your home or office that holds the energy of home, health, and family. This area is associated with active participation, new ideas, and reaching out, as well as physical and emotional healing and support.

Environment

Wood is the element associated with the east in feng shui. It represents spring, the beginning of the cycle of life. Wood contains growth, creation, and nourishment. Objects that reinforce this element in your environment include tall cylinders, rectangles, green floral patterns, plants, and flowers. Some schools of feng shui say that wood in your home or office must be living, such as small shrubs or bonsai trees. Others say that it is okay to include wood floors and furniture as an aspect of this element. The debate is whether dead wood counts or if wood must be living to contain balancing chi. In all things feng shui, trust your intuition. I have wood floors in my home and for a while I had an artificial tree. I am not a strict feng shui practitioner. If it feels right, then go with it until it doesn't.

The color green is associated with the east and healing, prosperity, luck, fertility, and harmony. It is probably no coincidence that operating room scrubs are often green. I wonder if the physicians know they are using feng shui in the OR?

Practice
Consider the East Area of Your Space

Take a moment to look at the east area of your home, room, or office. Does it contain any wood elements? Is there anything green? Are there any blocks to the flow of energy, such as clutter? View the east or health area of your house or room and ask yourself:

- What is healing within this section of the room?
- What is here that does not reflect a sense of healing or family?
- Are there any living, growing plants here?

- When I look here, do I feel healthy? Or do I feel tension, restraint, conflict?

- Can I add green to this area?

Cures

Feng shui cures to increase health, healing, and family harmony involve the use of wood elements, the color green, auspicious symbols, and the belief that what you are doing is going to work!

When using cures in this area, affirm your positive intention to heal yourself or your family. Believe that the universe is energy and that thoughts, feelings, and objects can affect energy. Affirm that energy is now flowing freely in your body, your mind, and your environment. Affirm the power of energy to heal and relieve any condition that is currently distressing you. Focus your attention on the healing that is now occurring and the well-being that is coming into your life.

Clear out clutter in your mind as you first clear out clutter in the east area of your room or office. Look at the area and notice which things give you a sense of health, vitality, and healing and which do not. For example, if the east area of your home is the mud room and there are always discarded towels, dirty footwear, and other messes, notice how that makes you feel. Begin to rearrange the area to gain a sense of cleanliness, orderliness, and harmony. Bring in the wood element of this area by adding a living plant. Lucky bamboo, *Dracaena sanderiana*, is a small bamboo-like plant that lives in indirect sunlight and at extreme temperature ranges and only needs water to grow in, no soil. It is a perfect plant for the health area of a room or office because it invokes bamboo, which is wood yet green!

Another great place to use live wood is where your staircase empties into your doorway. This is considered negative chi in feng shui. The cure is to place a live, potted shrub at the bottom of the staircase. This enlivens the area and creates good chi.

In Chinese folklore, the dragon is associated with the east and the spirit of change and transformation, while the turtle is associated with longevity, strength, and endurance. Placing a small statue of a dragon or a turtle in the east area of your room will add the chi of long family life and harmony. There is even an object called a treasure turtle dragon that is often used in this area. This statue shows a turtle riding on the back of a dragon whose body is a turtle shell. Combined, the statue represents strength, goodness, and longevity for the family and the individual.

Include personal objects that reaffirm your intention for good health and family harmony in the east. Place a photo of your family on vacation, relaxing and enjoying each other in perfect health. Write out healing affirmations and pin them up. Make a collage of the most healing pictures and words you can find, frame it, and place it in the east. Be careful not to crowd the area. One or two objects that represent health and family will do nicely. Above all, keep the area neat, clean, healthy-looking, and healthy-feeling!

The Southeast: Wealth

The southeast is the area in your environment that represents wealth. It is associated with good fortune and moneymaking. Wealth is a symbol of abundant energy flow and the freedom to do what needs to be done in the service of self and others.

Environment

There is no single feng shui element associated with this area. In the transition between elements in the creative cycle, the wood of the east moves southeast to nourish the fire of the south. Combining these elements, one may say that the wood makes fire and promotes higher purpose, laughter, meeting new people, and embracing life.

The color associated with this area is purple, the color of nobility and royalty. The energy of the color purple includes aspects of spirituality, wisdom, honor, and psychic awareness. A little psychic awareness combined with wisdom may help in the acquiring of wealth!

Practice
Consider the Southeast Area of Your Space

Look at the southeast portion of your home, room, or office. Does anything in it remind you of wealth currently? Is there any room to receive wealth? Any open spaces? Any signs of flow and movement? Is there any hint of purple or its tones of violet and indigo? Analyze this area for anything that feels to you like it is blocking wealth and for anything that seems to be attracting wealth. I know this sounds subjective, but energy, like the wind, is very subjective. We cannot see the air, but we can feel it as a breeze gently caresses our cheeks. We cannot see the energy of wealth, but we know the instant we feel rich—just as we know the instant that we feel poor.

Answer the following questions while viewing this area of your home, business, or room. View the southeast or wealth area of your house or room and ask yourself the following:

- What is here that makes me feel wealthy and abundant?
- What here makes me feel lacking?
- Is there space for wealth to come in here? Or is this area too crowded to receive wealth?
- Can I add touches of purple here?

Cures

Feng shui has many cures for wealth. Again, use a cure with the intention to help you change your belief about your relationship to wealth. Let each change you make in your wealth area reflect new beliefs about abundance and wealth coming to you easily and quickly.

Feng shui cures involve attracting wealth to you rather than getting wealth by effort and activity. They are symbols that remind you to allow wealth and abundance to flow easily into your life.

For good fortune and moneymaking, place a prosperity frog, a three-legged toad statue, in your wealth area. The origins of this belief date back to the tenth century in China, when the Minister of State Liu Hai was said to have possessed a three-legged toad that would convey him to any place he wished to go. To retain the toad, he would bait a line with gold coins and the toad would always return to him. Today the toad or frog represents auspicious symbols of abundance and prosperity.

Ever wonder why Chinese restaurants have fish aquariums and statues of Buddhas and cats by the cash register? The fish is included as one of the auspicious signs on the footprints of the Buddha and signifies freedom of restraints or obstructions. Live fish, swimming in aquariums, represent the flow of wealth and money and career success. Figures of Buddha laughing remind us to keep our sense of humor even in times of financial trouble. Buddha is often represented as traveling across the country with a sack on his back or sitting in bowl of plenty, always spreading joy, prosperity, and happiness. Lucky cats, holding the Chinese symbols for good fortune and wealth, are often placed near a cash register. In China, the cat is a natural protector of silkworms and therefore a source of financial success in business. Lucky cats are said to bring prosperity to any home or business.

Additional feng shui cures to attract money include the use of lucky red envelopes and ancient Chinese coins. Originally, Chinese coins were used as amulets of protection against negative energy. They became symbols of energy as they were used for money, just like money is used today. According to legend, placing three or five Chinese coins in a red envelope and then placing the envelope in your wealth area will attract money to you. Adding a personal affirmation of your willingness to receive money will enhance the energy. It is certainly worth a try, don't you think?

Finally, view the wealth area of your home or business with an eye for the things that represent wealth to you. What objects make you feel wealthy by just looking at them? They need not be expensive objects, but they must generate the energy of wealth and money. My favorite aunt and uncle were wealthy, or at least wealthy to me. They lived in a wonderful home with lots of rooms to explore on wooded acres of land. I received one item after their death, a brass stamp holder sitting on top of a marble base. That stamp holder was always on my uncle's desk in his home office. It represents wealth to me because it was his and he used it to grow a successful business. I recently found the stamp holder in a box that I had not unpacked for years and years. The holder is now firmly in place in the wealth area of my business. Each time I look at it, I feel wealthy. Find an object the helps you feel wealthy and view it often!

Another energy technique is to pile money on top of a mirror. Use loose change and paper bills. Allow the reflection in the mirror to multiply your money. As with all areas, be sure your wealth area is free of clutter, neat and clean. Allow some emptiness so that there is space to receive money. Relax and enjoy money flowing into your life.

The South: Fame and Success

The south represents the area in your home or office that holds the energy of fame and success. This area is associated with enthusiasm, courage, vitality, and good fortune.

Environment

Fire is the element associated with the south in feng shui. Fire represents life energy and action. It is the summer, the peak of the natural cycle. Objects that reinforce this element include triangular, pointed, and angular shapes and red designs in fabrics, carpets, and artwork. The use of candles, incense, and sage smoke also introduces the element of fire into the environment.

The color red is associated with your fame and success area. Red represents love, passion, and energy and attracts recognition, respect, confidence, and luck. Red aids in motivation and inspiration, open-heartedness, fun, laughter, and networking. Variations of the color red are also appropriate for this area, including purple, the heart of fire, and orange.

Practice
Consider the South Area of Your Space

Look now at the south portion of your room, home, or business. Does it contain any of the elements of fire? Are there any candles or the color red anywhere? Does this area of your dwelling look successful? What reminds you of success when you look south? Hold these thoughts as we move on to beliefs. View the south or fame area of your house or room and ask yourself the following:

- What calls fame and attention here?
- Are there any candles here?
- What would put out the fire in this area?
- Can I add touches of red here?

Cures

First, clear all the clutter from the south/success area of your home, room, or business. Organize an area for work in this space. You may have a small table or simply a notepad where you can write down your ideas and plans for success. In feng shui, the work area is to be organized so you always face the door. It is believed that when your back is to the door, you are vulnerable and are inviting competition into your life.

You may also want to look at your front door, even if it is not in the south. Is the front of your business or home welcoming success, or are there barriers present? Clutter is one barrier. Dark or closed-in feelings around the door are another. Is the porch or steps leading to the door neat and clean, or are there uneven or broken places? Clearing, repairing, adding lights, and mirrors all beacon success.

Returning to the south portion of the room, try adding a red candle or a red rose (silk roses are fine), some incense, or other items that connect with the fire element. Make a collage of photos that remind you of success. Add personal treasures that bode success for you, remembering not to clutter the area. Have the intention of success each time you view this area. Feel the feeling of success each time you think about this area. Give yourself permission to be successful, no matter what anyone else says to you or even thinks about you. Know you are successful, and it will come.

The Southwest: Relationships

The southwest holds the energy of relationships, marriage, and business partnerships. It is associated with support, sharing, and selflessness.

Environment

No single feng shui element is associated with this area. It is the transition between the red of the fire element and the white of the metal element. The perfect blending of red and white produces pink. Pink is the color of emotional healing, protection, love, support, and letting go. In terms of energy, the white light from heaven merges with the red light of earth, blending, soothing, and harmonizing. Pink is often associated with the heart and loving.

Practice
Consider the Southwest Area of Your Space

Look at the southwest area of your home or office. What is there that reminds you of love? Again, look for clutter, dust, disorganization. Is your love dusty? If you are single, is there any space in this area to invite others into your life? If you are married or living with a partner, is there space for your relationship to unfold? Just note the changes you may wish to make in this area for now. View the southwest or relationship area of your house or room and ask yourself:

- What promotes good relationships here?
- What creates conflict in this area?

- What clutter here represents poor communications in relationships?
- Can I add touches of pink here?

Cures

The first cure for relationships is to love yourself unconditionally. If you place conditions on your own self-love, then you will place conditions on the love you give to others. If you only love yourself when you accomplish something, when you are healthy, or when you do good, then you must, by default, apply that criterion to those around you. Practice loving yourself when you feel bad, when you have just made a mistake, when you have been unkind. Practice loving yourself because you exist, because you are living, because you are here. Meditation will assist you in developing the feelings of unconditional love. The more you understand the transitory nature of reality, the more you will come to know that just being here is enough. Just loving is enough. And when you are full of love inside, it naturally overflows into your relationships and the world. Give yourself permission to love yourself. And then expand that permission to loving others. Being in relationships with others unconditionally will bring good chi into your life.

On the more tangible side, feng shui includes cures to enhance these feelings of love and relationship. In the southwest area of your room or business, place pairs of things to remind you that you are in a relationship, even if that relationship is only between you and your cat! Find two matching candles, pink in color, and set them together. Two Austrian crystals hanging side by side, equally matched, will bring relationship chi into your area. Two matching mirrors, two matching cushions, or two of anything peaceful and loving will do nicely.

Fish tanks or carvings of fish are often placed in this area. In China, the carp fish represents harmony and marital bliss, especially when two of them are seen swimming together against the current. Facing obstacles together has become an emblem of perseverance. The fish symbol may be used in a business or office to enhance relationships between employees and customers.

Since we are on the relationships area, we need to discuss the arrangement of your bedroom—even if it is not in the southwest of your home. For successful relationships, place the head of the bed against a wall and centered, so that both people can get in without a struggle. The ideal location is to place the bed so you have a clear view of the door from the bed, but not directly in front of a door. In the bedroom, use pairs of things to enhance relationships. Matching night tables on both sides of the bed, matching lights, and matching pillows all enhance the energy of relationships.

Finally, in the bedroom, feel free to say, and mean, "I love you" as the last thing at night and the first thing in the morning. "Good night, I love you!" and "Good morning, I love you!"

The West: Creativity and Children

The west represents children and creativity. It is associated with intuition, organization, and completing things. We raise our children and then let them go. We complete our projects and then move on to something else. And we listen to our inner voice of intuition to know when to apply our talents to the next cycle.

Environment

The west is associated with the season of autumn, the waning of the natural cycle, the middle years of life. A time of finishing things by the development of self-discipline accompanied by creative ways to handle life. The element metal is used in the west to bring the energy of completion and success. Try metal frames, brass doorknobs, sculptures, domes, cylinders, and round shapes. Metal is the most common remedy for negative earth energies. The use of copper, silver, gold, and bronze balance and bring harmony. Use of the colors white, silver, gold, and metallic is included in the west. The color white is a blank canvas, on which to paint your picture of creativity and fruition. Fun objects, childlike objects, games, and toys are all appropriate for the west. In our store in the children and creativity section we have fairies, Smoky Mountain trolls, and wizards, among things that remind us to enjoy, be in awe, and have fun.

Practice
Consider the West Area of Your Space

Look at the west of your room or home and seek out the fun. What is creative there? What makes you smile? What reminds you to be young and adventurous? Children live in the now, moment to moment. They draw tremendous creativity from their minds and imaginations. The energy of this area invites you to explore your own creativity and to have fun.

View the west or children and creativity area of your house or room and ask yourself the following:

- What is playful and creative in this area?
- What blocks creativity in this area?
- Is the clutter here creative or just messy?
- Can I add touches of white here?

Cures

To bring the energy of creativity, and creation, into your home or office, hang a crystal in a window. The most common hanging crystals are made of leaded glass. The microscopic particles of lead catch the rays of the sun, reflecting them into rainbows across the room. Austrian crystals do nicely and come in a variety of shapes. Crystals draw active yang active energy into your environment and promote the energy for completion of projects. The miracle of watching rainbows appear in your room as the sun shines through brings an instant sense of wonder and awe to any environment.

Look at the creativity area of your room and add small, whimsical touches. Maybe a stature of a fairy or a four-leaf clover. Perhaps a childhood toy or a new creative project can occupy a special space. Bring in objects that remind you to be childlike and to have fun. In a more sophisticated setting, such as a professional office, use the metal element in the form of statures, figurines, or furniture to enhance the energy of this area. Play with this wonderful energy of children and creativity and experience youth and energy returning to you daily.

The Northwest: Helping People

The northwest is the area in your environment that represents giving and receiving—helping people. It is the hospitality area, and its energy promotes natural caring and kindness.

Environment

This area is the transition between the white of creativity and the black of career. Its color is gray, representing protection and mutual caring. A sharing of resources occurs here. The energy is related to commitment, pride, and dedication. Neither black nor white, there is room for flexibility and growth.

In our store, we have placed our hospitality feature in this area. We offer coffee, tea, water, and other beverages to our customers. It represents a gesture of caring, of giving and receiving that enhances the energy of the entire store.

Practice
Consider the Northwest Area of Your Space

Look at the helping people area of your home or business now. What is there to remind you of sharing and caring? What attracts and benefits? What repels and limits? View the northwest or helping people area of your house or room and ask yourself the following:

- What is here that could help another person?
- What is here that is preventing me from helping others?
- Can I add the color gray anywhere here?

Cures

The most notable cure for the area of helping people is the use of mirrors. What we give to a mirror is reflected directly back to us. The mirror is a symbol for giving and receiving.

In feng shui, mirrors are used in two ways. First, they are used to reflect negativity away from an area. The eight-sided baqua mirror is often hung on a door to reflect negative outside energy back before it is received inside. Traditionally, mirrors have been hung on doors that face cemeteries, power lines, traffic, negative neighbors, trash piles, and so on. This is so that what is given from the outside is not received into the home or office. In addition, mirrors are often used in apartment buildings to reflect the energies of your neighbors away. Placing a mirror face down on the floor will reflect the energy from below back down. The same is true when placing a mirror face up on the ceiling, to reflect energy upward. Mirrors placed on bathroom doors reflect energy away from going down the drain.

Mirrors may also be used to reflect positive energies inside. If your window looks out onto a park, trees, or a beautiful scene in nature, position a mirror so that the scene is reflected inside. Thus, you receive beauty inside your home or office.

It is obvious that cures using mirrors are not directly related to helping people. In fact, they appear to be pushing people and objects away. Yet indirectly they do help. Negativity that is reflected back to its source will provide a lesson to the source. In the case of people, the more negativity a person gives out, the more they receive, until they realize that there must be a better way. As we learn that the world is a reflection of our own thoughts and beliefs, we gain the power to change our world by changing what we are giving out. We look in the mirror and frown, and we receive a frown back. We look in the mirror and smile, and we receive a smile back. That is the lesson, and it is really quite simple. It just takes practice to learn. Happy giving and receiving.

The North: Career

The north is your career focus. Career represents your livelihood, line of business, and in some wonderful cases, your calling. When your career and your calling match, then you love what you are doing and what you are doing loves you!

Environment

Water is the element in the career section. Water is formless and flowing. It conforms to and takes the shape of its container yet seeks always to flow and expand. Water is the element that allows us to be in the flow and feel the energies that cycle through life. This flow of energy aids clarity and communication of our ideas into action.

Black is the color associated with the career section of our environment. Black is the energy of absorption, black holes, and destruction of negative energy. It provides emotional protection and power. It is associated with money, career, experience, depth, and income.

Practice
Consider the North Area of Your Space

Look now at the career section of your home or office. What suggests flow and advancement there? What appears to be blocking your flow? What career ideas are present or absent there? View the north or career area of your house or room and ask yourself the following:

- Is there anything flowing in this area?
- What is blocking a sense of flow here?
- What can be moved or rearranged to create a greater sense of flow?
- Can a table fountain or paintings with water in them be added here?
- Can I add any touches of the color black to this area?

Cures

The most obvious feng shui cure for the career area is use of the water element. Water reminds us to flow with our lives, to allow the flow of career and money to come to us. The use of table fountains is the most common way to enhance the energy in your career section. Water features are visual reminders of the constant circulation and pooling of energy, as water travels from the fountain bowl, through the pump, and over the fountain. Water fountains can be enhanced with special designs that remind you of your vocation and career. Water flowing in your career area allows you to grow and experiment in your job as you seek your vocation. And when you are in your vocation, it encourages the flow of money and abundance to come to you for your support.

Your fountain need not be elaborate. It only need have special meaning for you. Caring for your fountain, making sure it has plenty of water, and running it at least a little while each day becomes a metaphor for the caring you are doing in your career. Allowing the fountain to represent the energy of your career reminds you that both are beautiful, flowing, and working properly.

Look now at your career area and find a place to add water. If you do not care for fountains, perhaps a small aquarium will do. And if water is not appropriate to the area, how about a picture of water? Many Chinese restaurants have moving pictures of waterfalls or flowing rivers. With this imagery, they are allowing the energy of water into an area. They are reminding the viewer of the power of water to move all obstacles in its path and find the perfect flow. May water move all obstacles in your career path until you find yourself in the perfect flow.

The Northeast: Knowledge

The northeast holds the energy of knowledge. This area is associated with two different types of knowing. The first consists of facts and ideas. The second is direct, non-dualistic knowledge.

Environment

Water and wood combine in this area of knowledge. The color is blue-green, the colors of adventure and exploration combined with calming and relaxation. These colors of the sea and sky represent an openness to new ideas and insights.

This area of your home or business is a place for contemplation and learning. Use this area to explore new arenas of thought and act upon new perceptions.

Practice
Consider the Northeast Area of Your Space

Look at the northeast area of your environment now. Is there a place for comfortable reading? What colors are now present? How inviting does this area feel in terms of learning? Are you ready to explore your mind and the minds of others here? View the northeast or knowledge area of your house or room and ask yourself the following:

- Is there anything here that promotes a sense of knowledge and understanding?
- Are there any books here?
- Is there a sense of organization and knowing here?
- What can I clear out of here that seems to block knowledge or knowing?
- Can I add any touches of a blue-green color here?

Cures

Let the knowledge area of your home or office represent both facts and intuition. Use this area for books, audio recordings, and inspirational posters. Design a quiet reading space here, accompanied by proper lighting and gentle music.

Along with your books, include a notepad or diary in which to record your ideas and insights. This is a good area to use when writing your business plan or personal mission statement.

Enlighten the area with the use of eight-sided baqua mirrors. Allow the eight sides, plus the center, to bring you knowledge of the nine aspects of life. Expand your facts, give permission to your intuition, and find balance here.

The Center of Your Environment

The center of your environment holds the energy of nurturing, balance, and stability. It provides the feeling of total support from the universe and is the sum total of your choices.

Environment

Earth is the element associated with the center. Earth in feng shui is like the center of a wheel, the still point within that is necessary for steady progress, security, and caring. Earth is reliable, stable, solid, and confident. Earth endures endless change and remains itself.

The color yellow is associated with the center. Yellow represents longevity and acceptance of change through detachment. Yellow is a cheerful color. It opens and cleanses the mind and invites feelings of peaceful happiness and joyful bliss. Additional colors associated with the center are light yellow, beige, and tan.

Practice
Consider the Center Area of Your Space

Look now at the center of your home or room. Is there clutter, or is the space clear? Do the features seem stable and secure, or is there a sense of flightiness and instability? Is there anything in the center at all? View the center or earth area of your house or room and ask yourself the following:

- What is centering and stabilizing here?
- What is up in the air in this area?
- What gives comfort here?
- What can I trust in this area?

Cures

Make the center of your room a nurturing, healing space. If the center is empty, add an area accent rug in earth tones. Arrange clay pots with rich potting soil and live plants in this area. Use square-shaped objects.

Long, flat rooflines enhance the stability of the center. Ceilings at angles are thought to create negative chi. Bamboo flutes hung in pairs from the ceiling balance sharp angles or beams, deflecting negative energy and recharging positive energy.

Small wind chimes hung from the ceiling will also enhance the peaceful energy of earth. These chimes may sound in the breeze from ceiling fans or air-conditioning ducts. Use objects that remind you to be still and listen to the inner voice that always guides you to peace.

The Creative and Destructive Orders

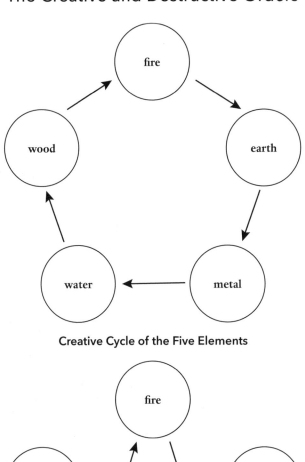

Creative Cycle of the Five Elements

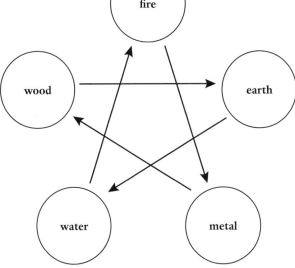

Deconstructive Cycle of the Five Elements

The five elements in feng shui have creative and destructive orders in relationship to each other. The creative order follows the seasons and cycles of nature. The destructive order attempts to go against natural cycles. It is believed that using the elements in proper balance enhances one's fortune, while imbalance blocks good fortune. To provide a proper balance, first eliminate areas where the elements are being used in a destructive way, then combine elements according to the suggestions that follow.

Using the Elements in Combination

Wood: Wood is nourished by water, as water is necessary for wood to grow. It is weakened by metal, as metal cuts wood. To improve health and family affairs, use fountains with growing plants. Contain water in resin or ceramic bowls rather than metal containers. Avoid using sharp, angular, metallic objects in the health and family area. Combining the colors green and black will enhance wood energy. A black vase holding a lucky bamboo plant works well. Bonsai trees are commonly seen in black bowls. Be creative with these two colors, using gentle black accents on green furniture or black frames around photos or paintings of forests and trees. Let the growth of health be nourished by the water element in your life.

Fire: The fire of fame and success is weakened by water, as water extinguishes fire, and is nourished by wood, as wood provides fuel for fire to burn. To fan the fire of success in your environment, light candles safely contained in glass with wood bases. Avoid placing candles too close to water features. Combine the colors red and green to enhance success and fame—just like Christmas! Hang red tassels with green jade, called lucky ties, to remind you of fame and fortune. Make a success poster using red and green lettering. Paint a picture, or find one, that uses vibrant red and green colors. Allow the energy of health and family to nourish fame and fortune in your life.

Earth: Earth is made by fire and displaced by wood. Candles in clay pots, bowls of sand, and incense all enhance the centering and balance of earth. Reds, pinks, and yellows are colors that energize earth properties of balance, centering, and stillness. Have you ever noticed the colors of robes worn by Hindu and Buddhist monks? The robes are usually of silk or brilliant cotton and always combine shades of red, pink, orange, and yellow. That is a good example of the fire element nourishing earth. Try combining these colors in your own wardrobe and sense the difference. You will feel more stable, more grounded, and yet more vibrant when wearing these colors.

Metal: Metal is made by earth and melted by fire. To enhance creativity, combine earth and metal in sculptures, planters, and artistic creations. Using bright yellows and brilliant whites together spark the creative mind. Yellow sticky notes on white paper are often used in business to enhance creativity and new ideas.

Water: Water is carried by metal and stopped or dammed up by earth. To enhance one's career, flowing metal water sculptures are often placed outside of business buildings. Inside, even water fountains can bring the energy of chi to one's career. The striking colors of black and white are also career boosters. Is it any wonder that for the past several hundred years, the classic business attire for both men and women has been black with a white shirt or blouse? Try placing abstract art in black and white on your walls. Energize your own thought by printing notes to yourself using big typeface on white paper, of course.

Chi and the Elements

Chi is the expression of the energy force of life. Heaven chi governs the celestial cycles; earth chi governs the ground. House chi circulates through a dwelling, and human chi circulates through a person. The circulation of chi without blockages, physical or mental, provides good fortune.

Chi nourishes our bodies, our hearts, and our minds. The Chinese practice of chi gong is intended to circulate chi within the body and to exchange chi with the universe. *Chi* means "energy," and *gong* means "practice." The more freely chi circulates in our lives, the more success, prosperity, health, and harmony we experience. The secret to the flow of this energy is in letting go. May you always let go and feel the flow.

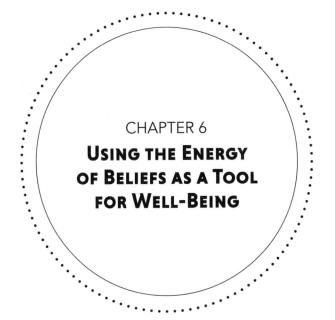

CHAPTER 6

USING THE ENERGY OF BELIEFS AS A TOOL FOR WELL-BEING

Beliefs are paradigms of encapsulated energy in the quantum field that affect our well-being. We believe our beliefs. We know they are true. We defend our beliefs. A paradigm is a collection of beliefs based upon our culture and society. They are the hidden assumptions our lives are based on. It once was believed that the body was a machine of solid working parts, separated from our consciousness, like the engine of a car. The belief now is that the body's energy is part of a far greater energy field. In quantum energy field theory, what we perceive as particles of matter are the excitations of the quantum field itself.[62] In essence, we, as well as everything we see and touch, are all vibrating bits of energy appearing as matter.

....

62. Viktor T. Toth, "What Is a Quantum Field, and How Does It Interact with Matter?," *Forbes*, December 20, 2017, https://www.forbes.com/sites/quora/2017/12/20/what -is-a-quantum-field-and-how-does-it-interact-with-matter/?sh=4c3d34d228c4.

Here is where the scientific theory of quantum energy meets the Eastern theory of universal energy called chi.

This chapter on the energy of beliefs combines my current beliefs in quantum energy with metaphysical beliefs in chi and universal energy. It is offered humbly as a new way to view your life and circumstances. Take what is helpful and moves you toward your own well-being, and disregard what you find stressful.

Beliefs about Health and Healing

Ultimately healing is an individual experience, combining multiple factors of body, mind, and spirit. All interventions, including pharmaceutical, herbal, surgical, bodywork, energy work, frequency, counseling, meditation, science, and religion, can move you in the direction of healing. On the physical level, disease occurs when there is a breakdown of the cellular membrane. This activates the immune system, as it plays a vital role in the biochemical healing of the body. Stress hormones decrease the functioning of the immune system. The less mental and emotional stress we place on the physical body, the easier it is for it to heal. You can meditate and still receive chemotherapy; in fact, meditation may actually help in the process.[63] It isn't an either/or modality choice. When facing a health challenge, you may consider using both conventional and complementary methods together as long as you let your primary care provider know what you are doing. For example, if your doctor prescribes certain medications and your herbalist has you taking herbal supplements and your acupuncturist prescribes some Chinese medicine cures, then they all need to know about what you are ingesting. It is your responsibility to tell them as part of your own management of your health care.

In 1987 Stephen Levine wrote a defining book titled *Healing into Life and Death*. The book was republished in 2010 after his death. Stephen's book came out of his experience in being with his wife as she was dying with a terminal diagnosis. It is possible that the ultimate healing is the return to our Source, to God, to love and light.[64] In Western society, we fear death instead of honoring it.

....

63. Stacy Simon, "Take a Moment With Meditation," American Cancer Society, June 2, 2020, https://www.cancer.org/latest-news/take-a-moment-with-meditation.html.
64. Stephen Levine, *Healing into Life and Death* (New York: Knopf, 2010).

Early on in my practice of polarity therapy, a client came to me with massive cancer tumors invading most body organs. She wasn't ready to die at that time, and the treatments I gave along with medical care allowed her to feel good enough to go back to work for a while. There she was able to complete some projects and say goodbye to her fellow workers who had become her friends. Then she began to, as they say, go downhill. It became too difficult for her to come to my clinic, and we agreed that I would go to her home. I was honored to be a part of the end of her life. As the visits progressed, I could tell that she was becoming more and more relaxed during each treatment. She passed away, with her family there, shortly after a treatment. I believe she was in well-being at the time of her death.

With the clarification that healing is broader to well-being than only getting better, let's move on to a new field of health, energy, and frequency healing. Energy-based treatments such as polarity therapy, reiki, therapeutic touch, and distant healing fall under the emerging collection of research in biofield science.[65] Current medicine sees the body as chemistry. Biofield science sees the body as a complex organizing field of energy that generates, maintains, and regulates the human body and the "body-mind as a macroscopic quantum system."[66]

If the body-mind is a complex quantum energy field, then our thoughts and beliefs must have an influence within that field. Earlier in this book we looked at research that demonstrated how stress affects the physical structures and chemicals of the body. Emotional stress may be transmitted directly to our cells through the vibrations of our quantum energy fields. Without taking a deep dive into physics, *quantum* "refers to a single packet of matter or energy" and "refers to the minimum amount of energy required for a change."[67] If our thoughts are energy and our bodies are energy, then what we think and believe can change our bodies.

....

65. Beverly Rubik et al., "Biofield Science and Healing: History, Terminology, and Concepts," *Global Advances in Health and Medicine* 4, suppl. (November 2015): 8–14, doi:10.7453/gahmj .2015.038.suppl.

66. Beverly Rubik et al., "Biofield Science and Healing," 8–14.

67. Anne Marie Helmenstine, "Quantum Definition in Physics and Chemistry," ThoughtCo., last modified August 9, 2019, https://www.thoughtco.com/definition-of-quantum-in -chemistry-605914.

Self-Inspection of Thought
to Clear Out Old Beliefs

Ask yourself, what would a person have to believe to be experiencing this, whatever this is? For example, if I am always getting sick when it rains, what beliefs do I have? First, I might believe that rain causes illness. Is that true? It's not true for everyone, but then why is it true for me? And because my beliefs, thoughts, and emotions can alter my body frequency and chemistry, maybe I get sick because I'm altering my immune system. And what would a person think who does not always get sick when it rains? Ah, maybe that person would not associate rain with being sick. Maybe I can decide to try and experience rain without getting sick and see what happens. Maybe I can let go of the belief that rain causes me to be sick. This type of thinking can go on for a while. If you work a bit at this self-inspection of thoughts, it may eventually allow you to let go of that limiting belief.

I am not telling you to ignore your body or forgo preventative medical checkups. I am also not saying that beliefs will provide a guaranteed or automatic health cure. I am only asking you to look at what you are reinforcing in your body. Your body does respond to your commands, especially when there is a firm belief behind them. Belief is thought combined with emotion. Why not tell your body something different?

Myrtle Fillmore, cofounder of Unity School, was told she was dying of multiple conditions and had six months to live. This was in the late 1800s, a time without modern medicine. She and her husband were already on a spiritual quest, and she decided to put her teachings into practice. Here is what she discovered, in her own words: "Then it flashed upon me that I might talk to the life in every part of my body and have it do just what I wanted. I began to teach my body and got marvelous results." Night after night, she told her liver how vigorous it was, her stomach how sweet it was, her limbs how strong they were, and her eyes how loving they were. She said she also stopped thinking any worry thoughts and stopped gossiping, among other things.[68] She used her faith, her belief in a higher power, continued her praises to her body, cured her conditions, and went on to live another forty-five years.

....

68. Myrtle Fillmore, "How I Found Health," *Unity Magazine*, 1897, https://www.unity.org/article/how-i-found-health.

The world is full of wonderful miracles of energy when we believe and trust a higher power and deeper wise self. Or in more scientific terms we shift our quantum fields, and the physical body responds. Belief works because we are energy beings at our core.

Practice
Believe in Your Healing

This is a short, simple practice that can be very effective when done at least daily.

1. Develop a phrase or affirmation you can repeat to every body part. The one I use is "Life in my _____ (insert body part), I love you. I release you. I set you free. So you may function perfectly. As (God, Source, or Creator) intended you to be."

2. Select a body part or say this to every body part. For example, "Life in my eyes, I love you. I release you. I set you free. So you may function perfectly. As God intended you to be."

3. Release any worry. Send light and love to the body part whenever you start to worry about it. Instead of saying, "Oh, my eyes are getting weaker," say, "I'm sending light and love to strengthen my eyes, and they are getting stronger." Why affirm the negative, getting weaker, when with the same thought we can affirm the positive, getting stronger? It's a matter of becoming aware of what we are already affirming and changing it if we choose.

Beliefs about Scarcity and Abundance

Do you believe in the law of scarcity or the law of abundance?

The law of scarcity holds that we live in a limited universe, on a limited planet, and in a limited life based on the sheer good will of others or on the fortunes of fate. At any time, what we have may be taken from us, depending entirely on the greed of others. The stock market falls, our boss fires us using the politically correct term of *downsizing*, and our funds dry up. And there is no more because there is only a limited amount for everyone, and we seem to have used up our share.

The law of abundance holds that we live in an infinite universe, on a planet that is self-renewing and has enough arable land to feed all its inhabitants, and in a limitless life full of possibility and adventure. Our fortunes depend upon our abilities to let go of anxiety and worry and embrace the all-providing spirit of plenty.

The spirit of wealth and plenty is manifested as money, and money is a form of exchange. In itself, money means nothing. What it represents means everything. What does money mean to you? Does it mean freedom to go where you wish and do what you want? Does it mean security to provide a roof over your head and food to eat? Does it mean feeling important and successful? Whatever it means to you is at the core of your beliefs about money. The secret to wealth is to feel wealthy deep inside, whether you have money or not. Change your beliefs to feel that you are good enough to be wealthy or that you do deserve to be wealthy.

Belief in wealth, being able to attain wealth, is vital to having money. As you explored each of the nine areas of the baqua, you might have found at least one area that seems to be a core belief that is currently creating great obstacles for you. Money is my issue. Yours may be health or relationships or creativity. I believe that when we place ourselves in the position to confront our core lesson(s), we have firmly stepped onto the spiritual path. The path to wealth can be very spiritual. Lasting wealth and abundance require faith and trust and openness. They require that ability to hold money loosely, to risk fortunes because you know that eventually you will gain them back and even more. The road to riches is paved with many who try and try again, convinced that this time things will work out. They successfully turn their talents over to God, a Higher Source, Inner Wisdom, or whatever term they may use and allow themselves to be guided into wealth.

In my working lifetime, sometimes money has been abundant, then tight, then abundant. The income from the store and website has been great, then poor, then great. Money comes when we allow it to come into our lives. It comes when we step off the hose and allow it to flow. Money ebbs and flows. It scares us when it ebbs and excites us when it flows.

In our current society in the United States, money appears to be stuck at the top and not trickling down much. That will change, maybe not in my lifetime, but it will change as we move as a nation from beliefs in scarcity to beliefs in abundance. The more we can connect with our Higher Self, supraconsciousness, that part of us who knows who we are, why we are here on Earth, and what our mission is, the more our lives begin to flow. And with them the trust that I do and will have all the money I need at the time I need it, and even more. And so will you!

Practice
Attracting Abundance

1. Take out a sheet of paper, or open your computer, tablet, or smartphone to a blank screen.

2. Complete the following sentence: "I have an abundance of…" Write down all the things you currently have an abundance of. Write down whatever comes to mind. Some words that come to my mind are *bills, water, air, problems, life, worry,* and so on.

3. Now go back and look at the feelings of what you wrote. What does an abundance of bills feel like? Too much, overwhelming, too hard, depressing.

4. Apply those terms to the abundance you desire, and you have identified some of your deeper blocks to having wealth. Having an abundance of money would be too much, overwhelming, too hard, depressing.

5. Just completing steps 1 through 4 is enough practice to enable you to develop more self-awareness about wealth and money. If you wish, you can turn what you wrote in number 4 into affirmations. "I am now ready to handle too much money for a change!" Or "Acquiring money comes easy to me now."

Beliefs about Fame and Success

What are your beliefs about fame and success? The classic paradigm here is pessimism versus optimism. A pessimistic person is one who looks on the worst side of everything and who has the tendency to exaggerate in thought the evils of life. An optimistic person believes that things are all right and takes a cheerful and hopeful view of life. The optimist believes in the doctrine that all is for the best and has the habit of looking at the brighter side of life.

Now, you are probably thinking that you know many people who are successful pessimists. People who appear negative and yet are highly successful. But appearances can be deceiving. The truly successful person is an optimist deep down inside. He or she believes that they can and will succeed—and they do. The successful person is also a consistent person. That person has the ability to be of even mind and emotions regardless of the circumstances. They were okay yesterday, are okay today, and will be okay tomorrow.

In what areas of your life are you currently a success? Perhaps you are a successful parent, or artist, or businessperson. In what areas do you wish to become more successful? Look at these two areas side by side. What are the differences in your feelings between these two areas? Can you pinpoint the feeling that motivates each area, the area of success and the area of non-success? Feelings that motivate success come from beliefs that you can and will be able to do something or have something. Feelings that motivate failure come from feelings of lack and unworthiness, the underlying feeling of fear.

Practice
Believe in Your Success

Try this simple practice. Think about an area in which you wish to be more successful. Close your eyes and connect with the feelings you have when you picture success in the area. Now think about an area in your life in which you are now, or have been in the past, highly successful. Close your eyes again and think about the feelings you experience when you remember your success. Very gently, with eyes closed, transfer those successful feelings from the past to the success you desire in the future. Begin to feel the success coming to you. You will have completed the practice when you hold the same feelings about your future success as you have about your past success. Every time you think about the areas of success you desire, note your feelings—and bring forward into the present those joyous, awesome feelings of success from the past. By your consistent feelings of joy and confidence, success will come to you.

Beliefs about Love

The basic belief paradigm in this area is the experience of conditional versus unconditional love. Conditional love in relationships requires that when you do something for someone else, they reciprocate and do something for you. You love the person only if you have visible evidence of their returning love. You love them only when they follow certain unspoken rules you have about behaviors in a relationship. Many of us grew up with one or more parents whose love appeared conditional most of the time. Those of us who were accommodators simply learned the rules and obeyed them. Those who were more rebellious did not follow the rules and often felt rejected.

To gain insight, I looked back on the relationship between my mother and father. I always felt judged by my mother, never good enough to gain her approval. On the other hand, I always felt unconditional love from my father. He loved and supported me always, even when he admitted that he did not understand why I was doing something that he would not do. I watched him with my mother. And you know what? He loved her unconditionally too! He never judged, criticized, or made her feel unloved in any way. And yet I knew that he had some problems with the way she behaved at times. But his love was always at the forefront.

Unconditional love—what a revelation. It is about never withholding love because of circumstances, values, judgments, or beliefs. You may not like or appreciate what someone else is doing, but you can still have compassion for them and give your love to them.

In the movie *Kundun*, the authorized story of the life of the fourteenth Dalai Lama, one scene early in the movie illustrates this type of love. The Dalai Lama is five or six years old and has just been discovered by the monks who were searching for him. He is held in the arms of a monk, enfolded in his robes. As he looks up at the monk, he is told, "You are here to love all living things. Just love them, care for them, have compassion for them. As long as any living thing draws breath, wherever he shall be, there in compassion shall the buddha appear."[69]

What if every child born were held in loving arms and told that they were born to love and to be compassionate? What if every child knew they were loved because they exist? No other reason. They were loved and loving. That is all. What kind of a world would we witness if unconditional love were the dominant emotion?

Unconditional love does not mean allowing murder and crime and other horrors go on without notice. It does not mean jumping into bed with everyone. Unconditional love reaches past actions, which must be dealt with by society, to the core of love in every one of us. When that core is touched, miracles occur. Hate and violence breed from fear and lack of love. Unconditional love is applying the love we give our pets, and the love given back by our pets, to the people we live with, work with, and have interactions with daily. Unconditional love will transform relationships into effortless mutual benefit. That is the powerful chi in unconditional love.

69. Martin Scorsese, dir., *Kundun* (Burbank, CA: Buena Vista Pictures, 1997), 21:14–21:38.

Practice
Believe in Unconditional Love

1. Think of a pet or a person you love unconditionally. No matter what they say or do, you love them. Nothing they can do will stop you from loving them.

2. Catch the feeling of unconditional love and then look at yourself in a mirror or in the camera of a smartphone. Take a selfie and apply that feeling of love to yourself as you look into your own eyes.

3. From there say something to yourself using the same tone and feelings that you use with your pet or loved one.

4. Go back to the practice, believe in your healing, and speak your words to your body parts with that same feeling of unconditional love. You may find yourself saying, "I know, eyes. I put such a strain on you. I'm sorry. I love you. You're okay now. I love you."

5. As you go forward in your day, become aware of when you criticize yourself or doubt yourself and begin to modify your self-talk with love. If you forget, ask yourself how your pet or loved one would respond if you spoke to them the same way you speak to yourself without love. I find myself sometimes needing to tell myself that I will not scare myself today!

The events in our lives are neutral. They are just events. Our choice is how we respond to them, from fear or from love. When we act in fear, we make mistakes. When we act in love, we create miracles. May you be loved and loving always.

Beliefs about Creativity

Fear prevents creativity. Joy promotes creativity. Fear of failure, fear of being laughed at, and fear of not being good enough all contribute to lack of creativity. Joy in expression, joy in doing for the sake of doing, and joy in living all unleash creativity. What do you feel creative at? Perhaps it is cooking or gardening or crossword puzzles. How do you feel when you are being creative? You probably feel light, swift, focused, happy, in the zone. These words describe a deeper sense of confidence in knowing what to do or at least how to figure out what to do. Creativity comes in many forms and styles. Everyone is creative. Belief in your own abilities fosters creativity. Fear of judgment from others limits creativity.

To develop creativity is simple. Try something that you have always wanted to do and do it. Treat each mistake as a lesson you are learning and begin and begin again. That is the fun. That is the creative part. Doing something new and being satisfied just in the doing at first. You may uncover a computer nerd, an artist, or a chef hiding deep inside. Do not give up or listen to the judging voice. Just do it. You will be amazed at the results and at the fun you have had in the process.

Practice
Being Creative

The easiest way to play with creativity is to sit with a blank piece of paper and a pen or pencil. Just sit with it awhile and wait for an impulse to come. You may have an impulse to write or to draw or to scribble. You may have an impulse to shape the paper, as in origami paper folding. You may have an impulse to make a list of all the creative things you want to do to relax. Whatever you do is you being creative. Creativity comes out of blank space. It comes from our inner minds and flows into the outer world. That's what makes it limitless!

Beliefs about Helping Others

The belief paradigm we work with in helping people is the belief that if I give you something, then I have lost it versus the belief that giving opens me up to more receiving. It goes something like this. If I give you a smile or a hug, have I lost anything? Of course not. I have received a good feeling immediately in return. In fact, I had to have that good feeling before I gave it to you. If I did not have a smile, I could not have given it away. Now, what if I gave you something more material, let us say money? I give you ten dollars. Now you have my ten dollars and I apparently have it no more. But I have opened myself up to receiving it back from another source. That is the notion of tithing. When I give freely, it is because I know that I have it to give. And knowing that I have it to give, I am opening up my energies to receiving it back.

There is a catch. When I give with the feeling of sacrifice, I will receive sacrifice back. When I give with the feeling of abundance, I will receive abundance back. But do not look for it coming back necessarily from the same source. Giving and receiving is not indebtedness. It is not giving so someone will owe you something.

A Course in Miracles states that giving and receiving are the same.[70] What we give, we receive. And what we receive, we have given. That includes everything—attitudes, feelings, money, material objects—everything! We are giving and receiving all the time. When we give a smile, one comes back to us. When we give anger, it comes back to us. When we give money, it too comes back to us. We are teaching and learning by what we are giving and receiving.

Let this area of helpful people be your focus for giving only that which you wish to receive. To receive love, give it. To receive money, give it. To receive peace, give it. What are you giving today?

....

70. Schucman, *A Course in Miracles,* 89.

Practice
Helping People

1. On a sheet of paper make two columns, one titled "Giving," the other titled "Receiving."

2. First, fill in the giving column with what you are giving to help others. Include not only the charities to which you give money, but also the time you give to help others each day or week and the emotions you give to help others.

3. Next, fill in the receiving column. What are you receiving materially and emotionally from others?

4. Are your columns balanced? Do you like what you are receiving based on what you are giving?

5. Finally, ask yourself what you can do to balance for your highest good and the highest good of others. On airplanes the flight attendants always advise in case of emergency to put on your own oxygen mask first before helping others. If you are always giving and not taking care of yourself, then you are not giving your best to the person you are trying to help. If you need to, make some adjustments in your giving and receiving to enhance your well-being.

Beliefs about Work

The basic paradigm here is work to earn a living versus work as vocation and calling. In the real world, most of us are heavily tied to the belief that we must work to earn money. We will pursue our calling only after we have worked long enough and hard enough to retire. Then we will do what we really want to do.

Many people become dissatisfied with their jobs and attempt to make what they love to do profitable. Some succeed. Some fail. The difference between success and failure appears to lie in the core beliefs of the individual person. The best, and most risky, way to test your belief about job versus career is to pursue your dream. When you go for it, you will meet up directly with your fears. When you do not go for it, the universe will have a way to push you into your vocation, whether you want to go or not.

My husband and I had a plan. We were both physical therapists and planned to work at our respective jobs until we retired. Then we would pursue our calling of music and spiritual teaching and writing. In 1988 we were both employed by large corporations and living in Augusta, Georgia. An Indian swami came to Augusta, and we were invited to attend his concert. The spiritual energy of this man was tremendous. We spent a week with him, learning Kriya yoga and becoming spiritually energized. This was not something we actively sought out. We had at the time little interest in anything quite so esoteric.

The week after being with the swami, three things happened simultaneously. We visited the North Carolina mountains on vacation and, through an accident of fate, met a realtor who took us on our current property. We walked on the land and knew that we were supposed to buy it, but we did not have a clue how to pay for it or why we were buying it. Six weeks later we found ourselves closing on the land with no money down. The bank had put up 80 percent and the broker had put up the additional 20 percent. We returned to Augusta wondering what to do and received two phone calls. One was from a realtor who wanted to buy our home in Augusta (it had not been on the market), and the other was from a company who needed to hire two physical therapists for a hospital and home health agency ten miles from the land we had just purchased. The universe was telling us something, and we had to listen!

We moved to the mountains in 1994, still planning to work as physical therapists until we retired. That lasted about three years, and then the universe spoke again—in the form of being downsized from our jobs. At the same time, a small building on the major highway through the mountains became available for rent. The building was a half-mile from our home. We rented it and opened a storefront and learning center. There seemed to be no other spiritual choice. We were being placed in the position that our job could become our calling.

The years between then and now have been spiritually, and economically, challenging. The 2008 economic recession guided us to moving our store off the main highway and onto our property. We had converted three acres already to an outdoor public space, Labyrinth Park. Moving the storefront over to the park was perfect. Charlie found time to pursue his music creating and recording songs and YouTube videos. I did return to physical therapy, but this time as a PRN contract therapist, giving me time to earn money and still be at the store.

We both moved toward our vocations, our life callings. We spent the twists and bends in the river navigating together. But we knew, in a deep and knowing way, that each day we were flowing in the direction of our true purpose in this world. That is the meaning of *career*. Some people know what they are to do from birth and they just go and do it. Others, like us, stumble through all the old beliefs, clearing them one by one, until we finally reach the knowledge of who we are and what it is we are to do. Now, without Charlie, who made his transition to the light in 2020, I trust the flow to carry me through in my unexpected singlehood. Having the opportunity to revise this book from Llewellyn Worldwide is evidence of this flow working as I let go of the life I thought I would have and allow my life to move forward.

Practice
Beliefs about Work

Back to your blank sheet of paper again, or computer or smartphone or anything you can write on that is blank. For a moment I want you to visualize what you would do for your work if you could do or be anything you wanted. Imagine going through your day doing that thing. Where would you wake up? Where would you be living? What would you be doing and with whom during the day? What would you do in the evening? Be as specific as possible and let your imagination run wild.

1. Now write down as much as you remember from your mental visualization.

2. Below it, list all the reasons why you cannot do the kind of work that you want to do.

3. Look at the reasons you cannot do what you want to do and see if you can change any of them toward your goal. For example, if you want to teach music, is there a class you could take at a local community college that leads toward that goal?

4. And finally, allow Spirit to guide your steps toward being in the right place at the right time to make the right decisions that further propel you into the work you came here to do. Meditate on joy. Meditate on miracles. Meditate on receiving direction from Spirit. Then sit back and enjoy the ride!

Beliefs about Knowledge

The balance of beliefs here is relying on facts versus trusting intuition. All facts have beliefs and feelings associated with them. All facts change. A fact is considered something that is real and true at the time it was believed. It once was considered a fact that the world was flat. In today's world, facts are evolving, as both our science and our intuition grow in leaps and bounds.

Facts are different from intuition or direct knowing. Non-dualistic, choiceless awareness is associated with this type of knowledge. Some people know Creator. They do not just believe in God/Creator. They are not able to describe Creator in words. They simply know that God/Creator exists, is their Source, and is within them. This type of intuition or knowing guides our most profound actions. Examples abound of people who are driving down a familiar street and suddenly make an unexpected turn that appears illogical or not based on facts. Later they find out that if they had not made that turn, they would have been involved in a car accident or would have not discovered a new place to eat or relax. Following our intuition is equally as important as respecting the facts. Both must be in our lives.

Practice
Using a Pendulum to Connect with Inner Knowledge

Have you ever listed all the facts about why you should or shouldn't do something, then did the opposite? You followed your intuition. The next time you have a decision to make, add your Inner Wisdom into the picture of your pros and cons lists by using a pendulum.

1. Construct a pendulum. Take off a ring you are wearing and thread some string or even dental floss through it, so it is hanging down and able to swing freely. Hold loosely at the top of the string with your arm steady. You may need to put your elbow on a table and shorten the string so the ring moves freely. You now have a pendulum!

2. Gently hold the pendulum and first ask, "What is yes?" The pendulum will begin to move in one of many directions: back and forward, side to side, diagonal, clockwise, or counterclockwise. Establish the direction for yes, then ask, "What is no?"

3. Once you know the directions for yes and no, ask the pendulum only yes-or-no questions to receive mental, emotional, or spiritual insights.

I wouldn't bet the bank on just a pendulum answer. Our egos are quite able to mask the true answer unless we are quiet and honestly ask Inner Wisdom for help. But using a pendulum is a quick way to access your intuition.

Beliefs about Centering

The balance in the center of our beliefs is between activity and stillness. Often when we are feeling off center, our first tendency is to do something, anything, to fix the problem. There is an adage that says, "When in worry, fear, or doubt, run in circles, scream, and shout." Activity gives us the illusion that something is being done. Because we are being active, surely the universe will respond and help us. Unfortunately, frantic activity blocks the energy of the universe.

Thaddeus Golas, in his classic book *The Lazy Man's Guide to Enlightenment*, says that to live a quality life, we must vibrate higher, and he uses the word *higher* thirty times in his short book.[71] He is referring to higher in vibrations, higher in love. And going higher requires stillness. The ability to calm the mind through meditation is most crucial here. When the mind is calm and still, new insights emerge. Frequencies change. New ways to solve old problems become apparent.

There is tremendous energy in stillness. Clearing the mind allows new beliefs to enter. Clearing the mind allows the energy of the universe to come into our lives. Just as the wind in autumn sweeps away fallen leaves, the energy of stillness sweeps away obstacles in our lives.

Practice
Feeling Your Center

Sit quietly either cross-legged on the floor or on a chair. Breathe into your belly and out from your belly three times. Place your hands over your navel and focus your energy to a point in the center of your body, between your hands and your backbone. This is the dantian, the power center of your body.[72] Imagine a small ball of sparkling energy there. Notice its color. It will be any color you need more of to balance. Now breathe and bring energy from the earth below and the heaven above into this center. Bring in energy from your front and back into this sparking ball, watching it grow. Bring in energy from your left and right sides into this energy ball and see it grow further. Watch your energy ball grow until it the

71. Thaddeus Golas, *The Lazy Man's Guide to Enlightenment* (New York: Bantam Books, 1972; Layton, UT: Gibbs Smith, 2002), loc. 205, Kindle.
72. Lee Holden, "Connecting to the Center," Holden Qigong, June 22, 2018, https://www .holdenqigong.com/connecting-to-the-center/.

ball expands outward front and back, side to side, up and down, until you find yourself standing in the center of this wonderful energy ball of light and love. Safe and protected. Centered within your own energy frequencies. Now bring this fresh, clear energy back into your body, into the center between your hands and back. Send the energy up to your head and out to your fingertips. Down through your trunk filling every cell, tissue, and organ with pure, clean light and love. Down through your pelvis to your toes. Focus once more on your belly. See it as the center of a wheel and how clean and bright it is, waiting for you whenever you need centering in your day.

Everything Is Connected

We are a web of energy making connections through our fascial fibrotic system throughout the body. Imagine putting a rock in the bottom of a large fishing net. What happens to the net? Everything moves! Everything feels the strain of the rock at the bottom. That is the myofascial system that we can see in the body today.

Several years ago, I was working as a physical therapist in a hospital when one of the doctors came to me with acute low back pain. He wanted me to pop or crack his back so he could get pain relief. I told him I would help him, but he was too tense for spinal manipulation. I had him lie down and began working on his head and neck. He kept telling me that his pain was in his back. I kept saying "I know" and continued to work on his neck and shoulders. You see, the stuck energy was not in his low back; it was in his neck, which pulled on the low back—again, imagine a fishing net. I finished without spending more than five minutes on his low back—it was not ready to release yet because the energy was still beginning to flow in his neck and had not balanced enough to relieve all the pain. He looked at me like I was a very bad physical therapist and left. The next day as I walked into the hospital, the nurses at the nursing station all said I needed to go directly to the doctor's office. I took a breath and went in his office. He looked at me and sternly said, "What did you do to me yesterday?" I thought, "Oh here we go," and said, "What do you mean?" He broke out in a big smile and said that halfway home his back had released, and he hadn't had any more pain last night or all day. He asked, "How did you do it?"

I said, "It's all energy and it's all connected." He thought about it for a while and finally said "They didn't teach us that in medical school."

It is all connected. If you take away the skin, bones, organs, and the circulatory systems in the human body, you are left with the shape of the body as a netting or web. That shape is fed by frequencies and energies from the consciousness, from the environment, from our thoughts and emotions, from our actions, from the foods we eat, and from the beliefs we have. Nothing is rigid unless we make it so. Rigid attitudes, rigid postures, and rigid thinking create accidents and dis-ease in our bodies and our lives. The beauty is that we can also undo what we do not wish by allowing our lives to flow rather than always trying to hold on tightly.

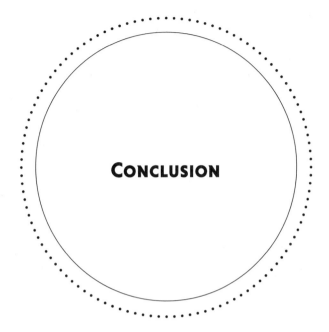

CONCLUSION

new paradigm is emerging, using words like *quantum physics, entanglement theories,* and *pulsed electromagnetic frequencies* based on the research in physics that began in the mid-twentieth century. Everything is a form of energy. Everything. Our bodies, our thoughts, the grass, the trees, the sky. And energy has frequency. We can no longer think of matter as separate from energy. What I feel affects you. And what you feel affects me. Have you ever walked into a room and immediately felt anxious, when just before you were happy? The frequency in the room changed your frequency. Have you thought about a person just before the phone rings and it's them on the other end? That's a frequency connection.

Well-being is everything and nothing. It is more than having a strong body but a worried mind. It is more than being an optimist but having everything in your world go wrong every single time. It is more than having hope but little faith. Well-being is the integration of and communication between body, mind, and spirit. It is calmness when things go wrong. It is smiling acceptance when things go right. It is having more moments of peace and joy and love in your life than not.

Abraham Maslow, father of transpersonal psychology, wrote that the big problems facing all of us are to make a good person, "the responsible-for-himself-and-his-own-evolution person," and to make a good society.[73] Now think again about the concept of well-being. How would you feel, what would you do, if you were a truly well being? Wouldn't you also be a good person? Wouldn't you take responsibility for your own life and not blame your circumstances on others? Wouldn't you be happy more than sad, loving more than angry, generous more than greedy, compassionate more than fearful? I believe you would. And what if we lived in a society of well beings? I believe that would be a good society too.

During my doctoral research, I discovered certain behaviors that are central to this ability to be a good person, a well being. The behaviors include the ability to experience life fully with total concentration, to make growth choices instead of fear choices by listening to your own Inner Wisdom, and to experience understanding and compassion for all living things.[74]

As you have worked with all the practices and exercises in this book, you have had the opportunity to directly experience shifts in your own energy. We all live together in a cosmic soup of energy. We are the ones who direct the energy that creates our experiences. We are consciousness who has a body while we live on this planet. We connect with that consciousness when our minds are quiet and allow the frequency of that rich inner wisdom to guide us, protect us, and keep us well.

I thank you so much for joining me on this journey. I hope that this book is just the beginning for you and that it becomes a quick reference as you move toward well-being. We are learning so much about the Unified Field of Consciousness, about how the body is literally created from this field, about how to tap into this field to change our thoughts and feelings and beliefs, our cells and even our DNA. We are all connected within this field, which is how prayer and distant "healing" work. It's the experience of the energy of the field that allows

....

73. Abraham H. Maslow, *The Farther Reaches of Human Nature* (New York: Viking Press, 1971), 19.
74. Jill N. Henry, "Development and Learning for Transformation: A Model Linking Lifelong Learning and Transpersonal Psychology" (doctoral diss., University of Georgia, 1988).

us to release unhealthy beliefs, the *I'm not good enough, I'm always victimized, I'm never in control* stored in our minds. When working with the energy body of a client, I can both see and feel the shift that occurs when an unhealthy belief is released. The body relaxes, the cells relax, and the immune system can now function optimally to rebalance the body. The future is exciting and open to reconnecting with our Source, Spirit, Soul on a level that enables us to find our purpose, learn our lessons, and do the work we came here to do. I am grateful for being given the opportunity to share some practices and theories in this book that may be helpful to your discovery of who you really are, a wonderous being of light and love. I thank you so much for joining me on this journey and continuing the journey on your own. The world needs you.

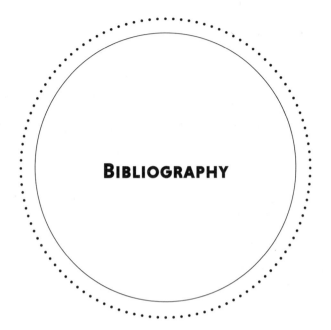

BIBLIOGRAPHY

Arias, Albert J., Karen Steinberg, Alok Banga, and Robert L. Trestman. "Systematic Review of the Efficacy of Meditation Techniques as Treatments for Medical Illness." *Journal of Alternate and Complementary Medicine* 12, no. 8 (October 2006): 817–32. doi:10.1089/acm.2006.12.817.

Bantornwan, Sirawit, Wattana B. Watanapa, Poungpetch Hussarin, Somruedee Chatsiricharoenkul, Nuttasith Larpparisuth, Tanyarat Teerapornlertratt, Jutamas Vareesangthip, and Kriengsak Vareesangthip. "Role of Meditation in Reducing Sympathetic Hyperactivity and Improving Quality of Life in Lupus Nephritis Patients with Chronic Kidney Disease." *Journal of the Medical Association of Thailand* 97, suppl. 3 (2014): S101–7. https://pubmed.ncbi.nlm.nih.gov/24772586/.

Benson, Herbert, and Miriam Z. Klipper. *The Relaxation Response.* New York: Avon Books, 1976.

Brook, Robert D., Lawrence J. Appel, Melvyn Rubenfire, Gbenga Ogedegbe, John D. Bisognano, William J. Elliott, and Flavio D. Fuchs. "Beyond Medications and Diet: Alternative Approaches to Lowering Blood Pressure; A Scientific Statement from the American Heart Association." *Hypertension* 61, no. 6 (2013): 1360–83. doi:10.1161/HYP.0b013e318293645f.

Burns, Jaimie L., Randolph M. Lee, and Lauren J. Brown. "Effect of Meditation on Self-Reported Measures of Stress, Anxiety, Depression, and Perfectionism in a College Population." *Journal of College Student Psychotherapy* 25 (2011): 132–44. doi:10.1080/87568225.2011.556947.

Carim-Todd, Laura, Suzanne H. Mitchel, and Barry S. Oken. "Mind-Body Practices: An Alternative, Drug-Free Treatment for Smoking Cessation?; A Systematic Review of the Literature." *Drug and Alcohol Dependence* 132, no. 3 (October 2013): 399–410. doi:10.1016/j.drugalcdep.2013.04.014.

Chitty, John, and Mary Louise Muller. *Energy Exercises: Easy Exercises for Health and Vitality.* Boulder, CO: Polarity Press, 1990.

Coué, Émile. *La Maîtrise de soi-même par l'autosuggestion consciente* [Self-Mastery through Conscious Autosuggestion]. Paris, 1922.

Dentico, Daniela et al. "Short Meditation Trainings Enhance Non-REM Sleep Low-Frequency Oscillations." *PLoS ONE* 11, no. 2 (2016): e0148961. doi:10.1371/journal.pone.0148961.

Dharma Khalsa, Singh. "Stress, Meditation, and Alzheimer's Disease Prevention: Where the Evidence Stands." *Journal of Alzheimer's Disease* 48, no. 1 (2015): 1–12. doi:10.3233/JAD-142766.

Elliott, James C., B. Alan Wallace, and Barry Giesbrecht. "A Week-Long Meditation Retreat Decouples Behavioral Measures of the Alerting and Executive Attention Networks." *Frontiers in Human Neuroscience* 8 (2014): 69. doi:10.3389/fnhum.2014.00069.

Golas, Thaddeus. *The Lazy Man's Guide to Enlightenment.* New York: Bantam Books, 1972.

Hay, Louise L. *You Can Heal Your Life.* Santa Monica, CA: Hay House, 1984.

Henry, Jill N. "Development and Learning for Transformation: A Model Linking Lifelong Learning and Transpersonal Psychology." Doctoral diss., University of Georgia, 1988.

Jacobs, Tonya L., Elissa S. Epel, Jue Lin, Elizabeth H. Blackburn, Owen M. Wolkowitz, David A. Bridwell, Anthony P. Zanesco et al. "Intensive Meditation Training, Immune Cell Telomerase Activity, and Psychological Mediators." *Psychoneuroendocrinology* 36, no. 5 (June 2011): 664–81. doi:10.1016/j.psyneuen.2010.09.010.

Jevning, R., R. K. Wallace, M. Beidebach. "The Physiology of Meditation: A Review; A Wakeful Hypometabolic Integrated Response." *Neuroscience Biobehavioral Review* 16, no. 3 (1992): 415–24. doi:10.1016/s0149-7634(05)80210-6.

Jones, Alex S. *Seven Mansions of Color.* Millbrook, Ontario: Cygnet Publications, 2015.

Jones, Laurie Beth. *The Path: Creating Your Mission Statement for Work and for Life.* New York City: Hachette Books, 1998.

Kabat-Zinn, Jon. *Full Catastrophe Living: Using the Wisdom of Your Body and Mind to Face Stress, Pain, and Illness.* Rev. ed. New York: Random House, 2013.

Levine, Stephen. *A Gradual Awakening.* New York: Anchor Books, 1989.

———. *Healing into Life and Death.* New York: Knopf, 2010.

Maslow, Abraham H. *The Farther Reaches of Human Nature.* New York: Viking Press, 1971.

Orme-Johnson, David W., Robert H. Schneider, Young D. Son, Sanford Nidich, and Zang-Hee Cho. "Neuroimaging of Meditation's Effect on Brain Reactivity to Pain." *Neuroreport* 17, no. 12 (August 2006): 1359–63. doi:10.1097/01.wnr.0000233094.67289.a8.

Peper, Erik, and Katherine H. Gibney. "A Teaching Strategy for Successful Hand Warming." *Somatics* 14, no. 1 (2003): 26–30. https://bio-medical.com/media/support/teaching_strategy_for_successful_hand_warming.pdf.

Radin, Dean, Marilyn Schlitz, and Christopher Baur. "Distant Healing Intention Therapies: An Overview of the Scientific Evidence." *Global Advances in Health and* Medicine 4, supplement (November 2015): 67–71. doi:10.7453 /gahmj.2015.012.suppl.

Rubik, Beverly, David Muehsam, Richard Hammerschlag, and Shamini Jain. "Biofield Science and Healing: History, Terminology, and Concepts." *Global Advances in Health and Medicine* 4, suppl. (November 2015): 8–14. doi:10.7453/gahmj.2015.038.suppl.

Schucman, Helen. *A Course in Miracles*. New York: Foundation for Inner Peace, 1975.

Scorsese, Martin, dir. *Kundun*. Burbank, CA: Buena Vista Pictures, 1997.

Srinivasan, Venkatramanujan. "Psychoactive Drugs, Pineal Gland and Affective Disorders." *Progress in Neuro-Psychopharmacology and Biological Psychiatry* 13, no. 5 (1989): 653–64. doi:10.1016/0278-5846(89)90052-3.

Stone, Randolph. *Health Building: The Conscious Art of Living Well*. Summertown, TN: CRCS Wellness Books, 1985.

———. *Polarity Therapy: The Complete Collected Works*. 2 vols. Summertown, TN: CRCS Wellness Books, 1986 and 1999.

Tooley, Gregory A., Stuart M. Armstrong, Trevor R. Norman, and Avni Sali. "Acute Increases in Night-time Plasma Melatonin Levels Following a Period of Meditation." *Biological Psychology* 53, no. 1 (2000): 69–78. doi:10.1016 /S0301-0511(00)00035-1.

Vyas, Rashmi, and Nirupama Dikshit. "Effect of Meditation on Respiratory System, Cardiovascular System and Lipid Profile." *Indian Journal of Physiology and Pharmacology* 46, no. 4 (2002): 487–91. https://pubmed.ncbi.nlm .nih.gov/12683226/.

Wang, Danny J., Hengyi Rao, Marc Korczykowski, Nancy Wintering, John Pluta, Dharma Singh Khalsa, and Andrew B. Newberg. "Cerebral Blood Flow Changes Associated with Different Meditation Practices and Perceived Depth of Meditation." *Psychiatry Research* 191, no. 1 (2011): 60–7, doi:10.1016/j.pscychresns.2010.09.011.

Zemach-Bersi, David. *Relaxercise: The Easy New Way to Health and Fitness.* San Francisco: Harper One, 2016. Kindle.

RECOMMENDED
RESOURCES

Chapter 1: Understanding the Energy of Stress in Order to Find Relaxation

- Chi-Lel Qigong, https://www.lukechanchilel.com/

    Master Luke Chan teaches a form of Chi-Lel Qigong that incorporates affirmations and gentle absorb/release methods in a large number of gongs or practices. You may search YouTube for free videos or enroll as a student online at the above link to gain access to all his teaching videos. I had the pleasure of working directly with him years ago when he was teaching in the United States and highly recommend any of his works.

Chapter 2: Using Meditation as a Tool for Change

- Insight Timer, https://insighttimer.com/

    I know it is sometimes hard to get going on meditation if you are by yourself without a live teacher. The best meditation tool I can recommend is a free app called Insight Timer. It is available at the link above or in your smartphone app store. Insight Timer has more than a hundred thousand guided meditations, eleven thousand teachers, and a singing bowl timer for mindfulness meditation. I use it daily for one or all the basic types of meditation described in this book. It's a grand way to begin!

Chapter 3: Exploring the Energy of the Chakras

- Henry, Jill, and Charles Henry. "10 Min Chakra TuneUp for Body, Mind & Spirit." WellBeingAtMVC, February 24, 2003. Video, 10:15. https://youtu .be/3JvTBr4_2DA.

  For an overview of the chakras, watch this video from my YouTube channel. My husband and I made this video to provide a quick access to tune up the energies of the chakras with words, colors, and sound. The script for it is written out in the chakra section of this book.

- Henry, Jill. "Solfeggio Chakra Tune-Up." WellBeingAtMVC, March 3, 2017. Video, 2:15. https://youtu.be/zUNmS-oE-fA.

  This is a video of all the Solfeggio sounds discussed in this chapter in two minutes.

  I'm also including links to the thirty-second videos for a more in-depth experience:

  - Henry, Jill. "30 Second Root Chakra Tune Up." WellBeingAtMVC, March 29, 2017. Video, 0:29. https://youtu.be/MQA2XFdQWTc.
  - Henry, Jill. "30 Second Sacral Chakra Solfeggio." WellBeingAtMVC, March 30, 2017. Video, 0:30. https://youtu.be/02kADAxfcRE.
  - Henry, Jill. "30 Second Solar Plexus Chakra Tune Up." WellBeingAtMVC, March 30, 2017. Video, 0:30. https://youtu.be/G7vWuNoBSqI.
  - Henry, Jill. "30 Second Heart Chakra Tune Up." WellBeingAtMVC, March 30, 2017. Video, 0:30. https://youtu.be/azrD8pp5Dgw.
  - Henry, Jill. "30 Second Throat Chakra Tune Up." WellBeingAtMVC, March 30, 2017. Video, 0:30. https://youtu.be/h-dQRfCe7zc.
  - Henry, Jill. "30 Second Brow Chakra Tune Up." WellBeingAtMVC, March 30, 2017. Video, 0:30. https://youtu.be/NC3OYdHz5EY.
  - Henry, Jill. "30 Second Crown Chakra Tune Up." WellBeingAtMVC, March 30, 2017. Video, 0:30. https://youtu.be/3tIElakRzfY.

Chapter 4: Working with Your Mind-Body Type to Balance Energy

- Henry, Jill. "The 5 Elements of Well Being." WellBeingAtMVC, March 14, 2017. Video, 2:08. https://youtu.be/3ub4sN-S-cw.

    This is a two-minute overview of the five elements discussed in this chapter.

- Henry, Jill, and Charles Henry. "Balancing the 5 Elements Guided Imagery 15Min." WellBeingAtMVC, August 7, 2015. Video, 16:34. https://youtu.be/VNe0bHPEDkQ.

    This is a fifteen-minute guided visualization to balance the five elements of earth, water, fire, air, and ether. Designed to release negative energy and allow positive energy to enter your whole being.

Chapter 6: Using the Energy of Beliefs as a Tool for Well-Being

- Henry, Jill, and Charles Henry. "Shift Energy to Health." WellBeingAtMVC, August 14, 2015. Video, 21:16. https://youtu.be/qV3rbD7Vxb8.

    For more information on beliefs about health and healing, watch our twenty-minute guided imagery video designed to enable you to shift your energy and your frequency to attract and allow healing and health into your life.

- Henry, Jill. "Shift Energy to Wealth." WellBeingAtMVC, August 28, 2015. Video, 18:00. https://youtu.be/yX4I0WIakng.

    For more information on beliefs about scarcity and abundance, watch our eighteen-minute guided imagery video designed to enable you to shift your energy and your frequency to attract and allow healing and health into your life.

Conclusion

These are a few bonus music videos that convey the message of the book. The first is a video to remind you who you are, and the second is a blessing to you and the world.

- Henry, Charles. "CC Long—There Is Light." WellBeingAtMVC, March 22, 2012. Video, 4:58. https://youtu.be/_zydi8BUJs0.
- Henry, Charles. "May You Be Loved Blessing." WellBeingAtMVC, December 31, 2015. Video, 4:45. https://youtu.be/nHag2io4nkQ.

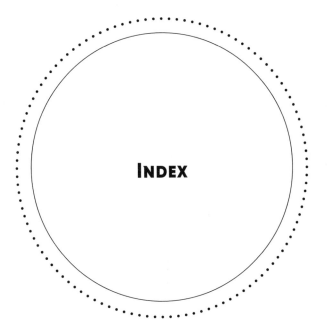

INDEX

To Write to the Author

If you wish to contact the author or would like more information about this book, please write to the author in care of Llewellyn Worldwide Ltd. and we will forward your request. Both the author and the publisher appreciate hearing from you and learning of your enjoyment of this book and how it has helped you. Llewellyn Worldwide Ltd. cannot guarantee that every letter written to the author can be answered, but all will be forwarded. Please write to:

Jill Henry
℅ Llewellyn Worldwide
2143 Wooddale Drive
Woodbury, MN 55125-2989

Please enclose a self-addressed stamped envelope for reply, or $1.00 to cover costs. If outside the U.S.A., enclose an international postal reply coupon.

Many of Llewellyn's authors have websites with additional information and resources. For more information, please visit our website at http://www.llewellyn.com.